Thomas Stone ★★★★

Elusive Maryland

~Signer~

John M. Wearmouth

Roberta J. Wearmouth

By
John M. Wearmouth
and
Roberta J. Wearmouth

Note of Acknowledgment and Gratitude

For their support of the Stone biography the authors are indebted to the family of the late John Digges Mitchell of LaPlata, Charles County, Maryland, in an almost incalculable degree. We and they fervently hope that this work will add a notable patina of luster to the heritage of one of Maryland's oldest, most distinguished communities. Thomas Stone, although greatness personified, was but a single distinguished personality in Charles County's little known but immeasurable contribution to the cause of our nationhood founding. Being well aware of this, Mr. Mitchell provided a legacy to be used in support of some worthy cause felt by his family likely to rekindle and advance a once almost universal respect for the nearly four centuries of Charles County, Maryland history . . . much of it having been experienced first-hand by John Digges Mitchell's antecedents.

Support for this work reflects the Mitchell family's desire to honor John Digges Mitchell's belief in a project that would revive and cast new light on the past of Charles County, Maryland.

Stones Throw Publishing
P. O. Box 296
Port Tobacco, Maryland 20677

Printed in the United States of America by Kirby Lithographic Co., Inc. Arlington, Virginia

Design by Stones Throw Publishing

ISBN 0-9719072-1-8

Table of Contents

Impression made by
Thomas Stone's
signet ring

now in possession
of Maryland
Historical Society.

List of Illustrations

Prefatory Note

If nothing else comes from this Stone work the authors have gained much insight into what it took to set our country afloat. The character of the main actors and their motivations that jerkily pushed them toward independence are difficult to understand today. Perhaps present society in America would not be up to a struggle such as that facing Thomas Stone and his peers from 1765 through the Continental Congresses of 1774 to 1781.

Laboring often under very real threats of total self-destruction (family, estates, business, health) the sometimes foundering fathers prevailed in a great pioneering, audacious effort to create a new social order in which each individual stood a fair chance to enjoy security, agreeable livelihood, freedom from oppression -- "Life, Liberty and the Pursuit of Happiness," words we hope are familiar to all Americans.

Our total satisfaction and greatly expanded knowledge about our nation's beginning has been generated by a decade of living with this work. The most disagreeable aspect was dealing with Stone's last months -- a most distressing time. Had he lived another decade he doubtless would have been thrilled and felt himself honored by early progress of the new nation. At least by 1797 the Stars and Stripes were noted and saluted wherever they flew over waters that licked the shores of the most powerful nation-states ever developed by western civilization. And their presence was noted with distress by the North African Barbary Coast emirs and sultans. And doesn't history come close to reflecting the past? Today's United States aircraft carriers and missile cruisers create great wakes in Mediterranean waters. These were once plowed, much more slowly, by early United States frigates cruising the same seas during the Napoleonic Naval Wars and Barbary State maritime depredations . . . all with incredible success noted both with respect and concern by Europe's major sea-power nations having traditional interests in the Mediterranean rim countries..

We have brought to bear in pursuing this biography the experiences of forty years living within 1,000 yards of the resting places of Margaret and Thomas. And we have attended many July 4th grave side services honoring the Signer. During the past four

1

decades we have seen and heard nothing that could possibly pay appropriate homage to Stone -- the courageous, deliberate and sensitive patriot who though always physically delicate possessed an inside toughness of soul and spirit that was never flaunted. Always intuitive, humble, diplomatic and insightful in treatment of his peers, Stone could be rigid and quite self defensive when conditions so demanded.

Even though the life and public contributions of Thomas are the primary purpose of this work, some details are included about other members of the family whose lives were intimately associated with Habre de Venture, the Stone home near Port Tobacco in southern Maryland.

As a recently introduced part of the National Park Service system the Habre de Venture setting offers the first opportunity for most Americans to meet Stone. It is true that Thomas accomplished no more than some other bright lights who led us to Independence. But few of his peers in the Continental Congresses left broader, clearer footprints along the paths leading toward the Constitutional Convention of 1787. And among his peers few have been less known and more neglected. The description of Habre de Venture is part of the tribute to his memory recently put into place by the American taxpayer.

The pages devoted to parts played at the Stone house by other family members seemed appropriate -- all related to Thomas but directly descended from Michael J. Stone, a younger brother. Between about 1787 and 1937 the old estate and its dependencies were managed by M. J. Stone and three descendants. During this period the original Robert Edge Pine 1785 oil portrait of Thomas was displayed in the old parlor. Another member was Judge Frederick Stone (co-defender of three Lincoln assassination conspirators) who lived at Habre de Venture (c. 1839-1845) and studied law there under his uncle William Briscoe Stone, son of M. J. Stone. In both 18th and 19th centuries Stone family lawyers held positions of honor and prestige in Maryland's judicial systems. Two served in the State's Court of Appeals.

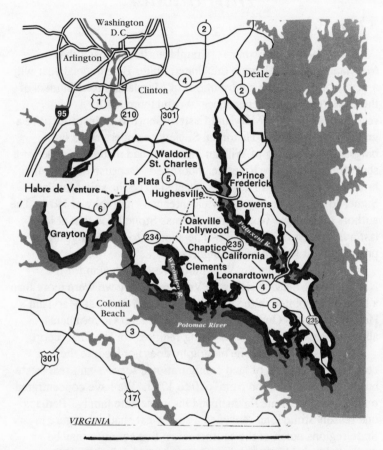

Habre de Venture neighborhood in the year 2002. Thirty miles south of the Nation's Capital City.

3

Part 1
Introduction

Purpose

In 1975 Mr. Arthur A. Houghton, Jr. proposed that Marylanders help celebrate the United States Bicentennial year with a new work about the contributions of Maryland's four Signers of the Declaration of Independence. With Houghton's recommendation the Maryland Eastern Shore Wye Institute gave a grant to the Maryland Historical Society to underwrite a brief biography on the life of William Paca who had made his home for a short time in the Wye River neighborhood. Because of this rather brief Wye connection Paca was selected to be the sole Maryland Signer to be honored by a new bicentennial biography in 1976. The authors of this new work about Thomas Stone hope that at long last a full measure of justice will be allotted to the youngest and probably least known of our Signers. [1]

In 1986, when the Wearmouth research began for the National Park Service Habre de Venture history we were more than a little disappointed in the very limited file on Stone at Maryland's Hall of Records. Our contract with the Federal Government allowed us two years for everything required for the final report.

This Thomas Stone biography does not include the considerable volume of land configurations, surveys and real estate business documentation from1680 to 1787. We have concentrated on highlighting Stone the man and his immediate family. Perhaps one reason Stone long remained a somewhat shadowy figure in State regions north of the southernmost five counties may be attributed to his birth and dwelling place, which had much more in common with States below the Potomac River than with the rest of Maryland.

As America entered the 19th Century Maryland's plantation-slavery counties became less and less important because of their peculiar economic structure and the steady drift northward and westward of the State's traditional geographical centers of wealth and political power. The southernmost Western Shore counties simply could not get into step with the rest of the State as industrial

---

1 Gregory A. Stiverson and Phebe R. Jacobsen, *William Paca, A Biography*. Baltimore, MD., 1976. Foreword.

revolution progress grew throughout other regions. Apparently the drifting apart of the counties even affected the State-wide perception of the very considerable role of Charles County in the Nation's founding and the cradling of the infant Nation before 1800. The stellar contributions of Charles County alone can easily match what northern Virginia counties contributed to the Revolutionary War-Independence achievements. Through the Federal Period Charles County helped promote national health and solidity. Actually, the five southernmost plantation counties held onto a rather significant political posture until the eve of the Civil War.

It is tragic now to note the lack of knowledge and interest of both students and teachers in American history. Curriculum designers must share the blame for this. How can Americans today truly respect and understand themselves without an intelligent view of the past that shaped their entire beings . . . whether or not their roots go back deeply in our past? Many cheapen the concept of patriotism that has given us much of our national strength and character. The tenets of patriotism still exist, but they need to be refreshed and enhanced by our homes and schools. Teachers of history through public grade schools, colleges **and** universities must be prepared on a learning level with any of their academic peers – history teachers are saddled with an extremely important charge – instilling respect for what had to be sacrificed by earlier Americans to allow us to be where and what we are today and armed to prepare for uncertain futures.

We trust this life of Thomas Stone will do much more than to simply profile one life spent wholeheartedly in the cause of freedom and democracy. Granted, the freedom was not permitted for all people in this new nation, but the Declaration of Independence was an earthshaking step forward for all peoples – possibly the French Revolution would have been delayed for years if the Americans (with much French help!) had not shown the way to dissolving ancient allegiances to absolutist monarchies abroad.

This biography should help Americans today comprehend the nature of the total human resources that characterized the leading colonial period personalities who brought forth in Philadelphia in 1776 a most remarkable, concise and inspiring document that united a very wobbly group of thirteen colonies. Each of the thirteen "mini-nations" was unique. There were many disparate interests – politically, socially and economically. New

England's many entrepreneurial manufactures and Puritan traditions had little in common with, for example, the slave-labor supported rice paddy agriculture of South Carolina. Concentration on the life of Stone brings with it the evolution of independence fervor during the decade before the break with the Crown. Interests and lack of certain colonial American common goals, and an unfolding development of attitudes about severing all connections with a despotic monarch and House of Parliament, come to front in discussions about Stone's changing stance on independence, and its acceptance by Maryland legislators sitting in Annapolis. There are many side-bars in this story that touch the piques, passions and contributions of revolutionaries from other Colonies. Among his peers in the Continental Congresses Stone stood tall and remained a substantial, politically astute and highly respected figure right up to the eve of his very tragic death at age 43.

The machinations within the Maryland State Assembly during the 1780-81 term are described herein. Historians for the most part are correct to say that Maryland's January 1781 Ratification of the Articles of Confederation has not been properly credited with its incalculable impact on our birth as a viable nation, under God and a properly empowered central government. It was Maryland's constant pressure between 1778 and 1781 that resulted in eventual resolution of the long irritating "Western Lands Issue." Leadership of Thomas Johnson in the House of Delegates and Thomas Stone in the Senate ended in a Maryland vote for ratification – **and** this led to meaningful French military and naval assistance later in 1781 that gained complete fulfillment at Yorktown on the 19th of October that year. And this was the event that shook a Georgian crown and gave the British "lobster back" infantry and grenadiers a memorable defeat of disastrous proportions previously unknown to them and the rest of the British Empire.

Stone had a front bench view of all these events. His old Port Tobacco and Frederick, Maryland neighbor, John Hanson, was the head of state for one year after Yorktown and therefore the first head of state of the new nation. The gallant Colonel Tench Tilghman handed the news of the British surrender on October 19, 1781 to Hanson's immediate predecessor. Stone maintained close surveillance over military affairs from the Lord Dunmore Chesapeake Bay depredations – the Montgomery-Arnold 1775 assault on Quebec – British blockade of Boston Harbor – Royal

Navy throttling excursions in the Bay and its major tributaries – and active support of Maryland's effort to prepare its militia for combat against British military forces nearly a year before the exciting broadside announcing Independence was released to public view.

The authors wish that those who read this work will do so in search of what our 18th century society contributed and risked on the way to independence. This resulted in a daring, questionable governing experiment that even now is only wished for by many countries and millions of people throughout the world.

Stone's life reflects a nature, background, ability and spirit for freedom not matched by most Colonials during the decade before the Declaration. He worked to help remove the wrinkles from government under the Articles of Confederation. He played a major part in marking out the spectacular trail from the Mount Vernon Convention of 1785 to the deliberations of the Constitutional Convention of 1787. This all really began with a highly diplomatic, skillfully crafted letter early in 1785 from Thomas Stone to George Washington, as ordered by Maryland's Governor William Paca. The letter indicated that Maryland was totally prepared to send delegates to Virginia in March that year to resolve ancient problems connected with sovereignty over and use of Chesapeake Bay and major tributary waters. Stone was part of this group at Mount Vernon.

The Boston Massacre of 1770, long before the Lexington-Concord clash, shaped emerging anti-Crown sentiments in all the Colonies.

Part II
Elusive Patriot
Greatness Misunderstood

It seems extraordinary that after more than two centuries since the death of Thomas Stone so little has been done to learn who he was and what he contributed to the Nation. Many Maryland people know that he was the youngest of the State's four Signers of the Declaration of Independence. But few Americans outside of his native State have ever heard of him. Historians continue to wish they could find a substantial, previously unknown cache of Thomas Stone personal papers so that something reasonably deep and broad might be discovered about this quiet lawyer, politician, legislator, and patriot who had few peers.

Even in his native Charles County in southern Maryland people still picture him as an elusive, not very substantial historic figure of rather unexciting proportions. In fact, Signer Stone left many scattered tracks over the pages of American Colonial and Revolutionary War period history. True enough, these tracks are not concentrated in a neat, tight little packet. They had to be traced patiently to many far-off sources and be brought back to his native county and State. Then they were fitted together slowly, carefully, and sympathetically to give him at least a fair measure of the recognition long denied.

An unforgivable example of the broad lack of respect for Stone in his native State and county lies in a letter written to the editor and published in the *Port Tobacco Times and Charles County Advertiser* issue of August 9, 1860 which suggests

> . . . that a suitable monument be erected on the
> town square in Port Tobacco in commemoration of
> the names of illustrious sons of Charles, who so
> bravely, so nobly offered their life's blood in
> defence of their country's rights. The names of
> General William Smallwood, General John
> Mitchell, Colonel Bruce, Captain John H. Stone,
> and others of our native county have been
> shamefully neglected upon the pages of historical

record . . . [2]

Type for the above item in the *Times* was hand-set in a Port Tobacco building about two miles from Stone's burial site at Habre de Venture. Then, as now, soldiers in fields of combat were at the base of a pyramid-type command relationship. At the very top were the truly great men of the Continental Congress who designed and ordered the military and naval operations in strategic and even tactical ways to implement the grand design that would either lead to independence or complete loss of all hope for ending ties with Great Britain forever. So, who were Maryland's great men of this period? Surely, Habre de Venture's Thomas Stone must be counted among them, even though his "uniform" probably was in somber tones of black, gray and white, as befitted a dignified young barrister-statesman of that time in Maryland.

For many years after the Revolutionary War General William Smallwood was seen by many Marylanders to be one of the State's most highly respected heroes. It seems then and now, that Americans more often than not really did think the sword and shot of battle far overshadowed the pen and ink contributions of the elite designers and innovators at the very top of the social structure. The appreciated, comprehended qualities of military leaders were often much easier for the public to grasp than the talents and accomplishments of civil-servant statesmen like Stone.

The feeling apparently was that Revolutionary War heroes were only those who carried muskets or swords or pulled cannon lanyards. Smallwood was not even present on the bloody Long Island field when the sacrificed "Maryland Line" bled almost to death as fresh, large bodies of professional British troops surrounded them, punching them into a helpless tangle, thus destroying the combat capability of a splendid body of Maryland troops – many from southern Maryland. [3]

---

2   Roberta J. Wearmouth, *Abstracts from Port Tobacco Times and Charles County Advertiser, Volume Two: 1855-1869*, Bowie, MD, 1991, p. 116.

3   Ross M. Kimmel, *Perspective: William Smallwood*, Annapolis, Md., 1976. The local call for a Smallwood monument to the memory of Charles County's foremost military hero came over half a century after Smallwood's death. William Smallwood, as a colonel, commanded Maryland's new nine-company infantry battalion organized late in 1775. At mid-1776 Smallwood's men marched toward New York at the orders of Congress. In August his Marylanders (a battalion of about 700 troops), joined Washington's main army on Manhattan and Long Islands. Starting the Long Island battle with a disease-ravaged battalion of about 400, the Maryland Line fought bravely and skillfully under the immediate command of Maryland's Major Mordecai Gist.

Earliest known depiction of Habre de Venture.. This representation is no doubt what William Briscoe Stone was familiar with when he began living here about 1820. Under his management the old house took on quite a new aspect until at about mid-19th century it presented a configuration that endured almost to mid-20th century. Sketch credited to Benson J. Lossing about 1830 in support of his work in American History. The Historical Society of Pennsylvania

Until recently Thomas Stone appeared irregularly and often in very uncomplimentary, dim light with questionable authority in a number of biographical sketches going back more than a century and a half. Beginning with the 1824 work by John Sanderson, *Biography of the Signers to the Declaration of Independence,* and continuing through the 1936 *Dictionary of American Biography,* Signer Stone appeared to have played a relatively insignificant and uninspiring role during the formative years of the Republic. There may be several reasons for such peculiar interpretations of Stone's contributions. One can hardly forgive Stone's younger, distinguished brothers -- John Hoskins and Michael Jenifer -- for not safeguarding their brother's personal papers upon his death. And then, the prominent Daniel of St. Thomas Jenifer had to have understood the merit of his nephew's contributions and should have taken steps to protect the Thomas Stone collection of private papers. In 1824 Sanderson wrote about Stone in his introduction that

> *It has happened, in respect to a few of those illustrious men* [the Signers] *that retiring when their noble task was performed, into the shade of private life, they soon became overlooked and forgotten by their compeers, whose earnest attention was engrossed with the consideration of the fearful events that were occurring near them, and in which were involved their own safety, property and freedom, as well as the honour and interests of their country.*

> *In such instances, the immediate friends have usually cherished the recollection of all the peculiarities in disposition or fortune that are ascribable to the retiring and modest patriot; and however barren of incident his life may have been, there is still something to be gathered with which a natural and rational curiosity may be gratified.*

> *But it has happened, with respect to Thomas Stone, that since his death, which occurred nearly forty years since, so many changes have taken place among his relatives and immediate friends, **that***

there is no one able, or willing, to describe his
particular habits, virtues or achievements, or to
testify the incidents of his short and unambitious
life.[4]

Use of the word "unambitious" here provides a clue about the slant of many of the brief descriptions of Stone that followed Sanderson's work. How could Stone's extremely demanding life from 1774 to almost through 1787 have been anything but a steady disclosure of almost unparalleled ambition? Time spent on the road by itself was then extremely dangerous and fatiguing. Stone's triangle of travel was Port Tobacco to Annapolis to Philadelphia and return. When his brother Frederick died in 1779 Stone hurried back to Poynton Manor to pay his last respects and returned to Congress. On top of all this, Stone kept two active law practices going 60 miles apart.

Stone misinformation passed along as being factual was published in the United States Department of the Interior, National Park Service publication *Signers of the Declaration* in 1973. This book was part of a series of historic places commemorating the signing two hundred years earlier. Presentation in this government book of Thomas the Signer awards him no more legitimate recognition than the descriptions of him printed during the previous century and a half. We quote to make our point: "By the time the Continental Congress voted for independence .... only a handful of conservatives remained in the body. Included in this body was Thomas Stone of Maryland. Stone, a rich planter-lawyer of retiring disposition preferred to stay in the background during his long but limited political career." [5]

The rest of the Stone material contains several errors –
. . . Stone . . . born at Poynton Manor . . . father's
plantation . . . enjoyed all the advantages that
accrued to the eldest son.

---

4   John Sanderson, *Biography of the Signers to the Declaration of Independence*, 9 vols. Philadelphia., 1824, 9:pp. 153-169. Hereinafter, *Sanderson*.

5   Robert G. Ferris, Editor, Washington, DC, 1973 *Signers of the Declaration of Independence: Historic Places Commemorating the Signing of the Declaration of Independence*; pp. 135, 136, 186-188, 189-191.

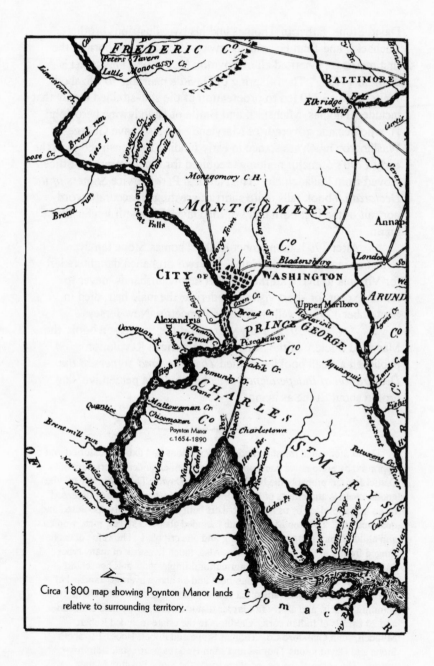

Circa 1800 map showing Poynton Manor lands relative to surrounding territory.

13

David Stone, father of Thomas and his two illustrious brothers, Michael J. and John H., married twice. Son Samuel, born of the first marriage, inherited all of Poynton Manor upon his father's death in 1773. [6] The offspring of David's marriage to Elizabeth Jenifer about 1740 led to procreation of the star-studded family that included Thomas, Michael J. and Battle of Brandywine hero John H. who became governor of Maryland. He also gave George Washington much assistance in early funding for construction in the early 1790's of major buildings required for the government offices moved from Philadelphia. The National Park Service *Signers of the Declaration* book falls quite short of creating an accurate word-portrait of the first born child of the David-Elizabeth Jenifer Stone union.

After 1793, no member of the Thomas Stone family remained in southern Maryland. His two orphaned daughters left for Virginia to live with their Daniel family husbands, never to return except for short visits. Frederick, the male heir, died in September 1793 of yellow fever in Princeton, New Jersey.

In 1912, many years after the Sanderson book, the Maryland Society of the Sons of the American Revolution published a small booklet entitled *The Maryland Signers of the Declaration of Independence,* which included a perceptive, fair profile about Stone as being

---

6   David Stone died intestate and his possessions had to be inventoried and appraised by prerogative court appointed gentlemen under supervision of Daniel Jenifer, probably the brother-in-law of David. This inventory of "the goods, chattles and effects of David Stone, late of Charles County deceased taken and appraised by us the subscribers being thereto legally appointed and qualified viz." Poynton Manor estate included about 65 slaves, men, women and children including a few suckling and one crippled. The value of each ranged from 1 to 50 English pounds. Also, much livestock of many types and an impressive assortment of agricultural implements and household goods reflecting a large, busy household and an above average standard of living – ½ dozen broken silver tea spoons, one silver watch and chain, two spinning wheels, and a very full larder that included 337 pounds of bacon and 20 barrels of Indian corn. Creditors to the estate included Robert Mundell, John Glassford Co., Thomas Stone and Robert Hooe. Elizabeth Stone and David's sons Thomas and John Hoskins were estate adminis-trators. The value of the slaves alone made the Stone Poynton Manor estate one of considerable value.

*rugged, reticent and reserved. Thomas Stone is
one of the least conspicuous of Maryland's great
Revolutionary heroes not because he was not
entitled to the plaudits of the enthusiasts of the
Republic then in the making, but because he
shunned notoriety, and it was only given to a few
intimate associates to know the true worth of the
man . . .* [7]

Most biographical notes on Thomas Stone picture him as a
quiet, cautious, ultra-conservative who signed the Declaration of
Independence with considerable reluctance. The truth seems to be
simply that a clear thinking Stone was able to put together a
rational balance sheet showing both the risks and advantages of
aiming for independence. In fact, Stone and the other Maryland
delegates at Philadelphia in the spring and early summer of 1776
were operating under uncompromising strictures placed on them by
the Convention of Maryland sitting in Annapolis. This body
governed Maryland after Royal Governor Robert Eden had been
eased out of power. The Convention, sitting safely in quiet,
provincial Annapolis, were afraid their delegates in Philadelphia
might not reflect the conservative Royalist stance of most members
of the Assembly. Late in 1775 the Assembly sent instructions to
their Philadelphia delegates pointing out that

*as upon the attainment of these great objects, we
shall think it our greatest happiness to be thus
firmly united to Great Britain, we think it proper to
instruct you, that should any proposition be happily
made by the Crown or Parliament, that may lead to
or lay a rational and probable ground for
reconciliation, you use your utmost endeavors to
cultivate and improve it into a happy settlement and
lasting amity . . . We further instruct you, that you
do not without the previous knowledge and
approbation of the Convention of this Province,
assent to any proposition to declare these Colonies*

---

7   The Maryland Society of the Sons of the American Revolution, *The
Maryland Signers of the Declaration of Independence--Their Homes and
Places of Burial,* 1912. (Unnumbered pages - section on Stone.)

independent of the Crown of Great Britain . . .[8]

From late 1775 to late June of 1776 the Maryland delegates had to represent their State within the rigid anti-revolution bounds prescribed by the Maryland Convention. No wonder, then, that Thomas Stone, and the other three Maryland delegates, acted on the whole with great caution while observing all about them in Philadelphia increasing agitation and warmth on the part of delegates from other Colonies toward supporting a complete break with Mother Britain.

Not until publication of the *Tercentenary History of Maryland* in 1925 did Thomas Stone receive long-due credit for being among those in the first line of Maryland patriots planning this Colony's initial effort to arm itself in anticipation of an all-out military confrontation with Crown military resources. Stone served on two committees established by the Maryland Convention to prepare for the apparent coming armed conflict. He was one of five distinguished patriots ordered to create a commissary department, and at the same time worked with another committee (including Thomas Johnson, Charles Carroll of Carrollton, Benjamin Rumsey and James Tilghman) ordered to produce new regulations to govern training and discipline of Maryland's militia soon to be raised for the Colony's contribution to the revolutionary armed force. The work of these committees was an indication that in spite of Maryland's perceived conservative stance opposing total rupture of her Colonial status her early actions to prepare for the worst reflected astute political realism of the moment – all in support of Maryland's early 1776 formal declaration of the principles of self government now seemingly violated by the very government that had long nurtured them for the well-being of all citizens of the British Empire. [9]

In a fair and refreshing change of pattern a concise but correct, balanced description of Stone's contributions appeared in the 1925 *Tercentenary History of Maryland,* Vol. IV:

He promptly espoused the cause of the colonies

---

8   *Sanderson, op.cit.,* 9: pp. 157, 158.

9   Matthew Page Andrews, *Tercentenary History of Maryland,* (Chicago-Baltimore, 1925, Vol. I, p. 548. Hereinafter, *Andrews.*

*when the quarrel with the mother country began,
and was a delegate to the Continental Congress
from 1775 to 1779 . . . During his terms in
Congress he was appointed to some of the most
important committees, notably the one designated
[in 1776] to draft the Articles of Confederation. On
May 15, 1776, he was one of those who voted for
the resolutions offered by Richard Henry Lee, 'that
the united colonies are, and of right, ought to be
free and independent states.' When Maryland's
delegates in Congress were freed from provincial
restrictions respecting ending of connections with
Britain Stone affixed his name to the Declaration
along with Maryland's other three delegates.* [10]

In Philip B. Perlman's 1948 article about Maryland lawyers
in Supreme Court history Thomas Stone received unforgivably
cavalier treatment compared to that given the other three Maryland
Signers. Stone was passingly described sparsely as " . . . born in
1743, one of the Signers." Faint, faint praise indeed for a man who
made major contributions to the founding of America and his home
State. Perlman proclaimed of the other Signers that Charles Carroll
was born in 1737, studied in the Temple Bar in 1757 and returned
to Maryland in 1765; William Paca was born in 1740, was a
graduate of the College of Philadelphia in 1759 and of the Middle
Temple in London, was Chief Justice of the State in 1778,
Governor in 1782, Judge of the United States District Court in
1789; and Samuel Chase was the "torch that lighted up the
Revolutionary flame," was born in 1741, Chief Justice of the State
in 1791, Justice of the United States Supreme Court in 1796. [11]

Stone, as the youngest Signer, was architect of the
Maryland Convention's executive arm, drafter of the Articles of
Confederation, pivotal player in the Mount Vernon Convention,
prime mover in the March 1781 Senate signing of the Articles of

---

10   Henry Fletcher Powell, compiler, *Tercentenary History of Maryland,*
Vol. IV. Chicago-Baltimore, 1925.

11   Philip B. Perlman, "Some Maryland Lawyers in Supreme Court History,"
The Maryland Historical Magazine, Vol. XLIII, No. 3, The Maryland
Historical Society, Baltimore, Md., September 1948, p. 190.

Confederation, long-time member of the Maryland Senate, legal counsel for the last Royal Governor in his suit against a Maryland citizen who had refused to obey Crown orders that everyone taxed pay toward support of the Church of England. And, in actual practice, Stone's education in the law under Thomas Johnson proved quite equal to that offered at London's Temple and Middle Temple Bar establishments. Stone's law practice increased dramatically between 1770 and 1787, both in his native Charles County and the sophisticated urban Annapolis world even as he struggled to balance his exhausting political support of the new central government and ever increasing demands of a growing private practice. There was in the 18th Century more than a little snobbery connected with European education as compared with less sophisticated education in the Colonies. However, the genius of Colonial professionals like Thomas Johnson and Dr. Benjamin Rush often at least equaled that offered in Europe's ancient, elite centers of Academia.

The 18th Century European education of some sons of the Colonial aristocracy often resulted in a disparaging snobbishness directed toward young lawyers and doctors whose expertise came directly from learning first hand from the skilled practices of masters of the learning arts as known then – here and abroad. Dr. James Craik, one of Colonial America's most renowned men of medicine, never acquired a degree in his art even though born and raised near the University of Edinburgh, one of Europe's oldest and preeminent universities offering the Doctor of Medicine degree. Craik served the Washington family faithfully and professionally from 1783 until he died in 1814.

The Stones of Maryland

Thomas Stone was part of the fourth generation of the Stone family of southern Maryland. He was a great-great-grandson of William Stone, third Proprietary Governor of Maryland, who was appointed by Leonard Calvert in 1648 to manage the colony's affairs from St. Mary's City. Stone served as governor from 1649 to 1654, after moving to Maryland from Virginia's Eastern Shore in 1648. He came at the invitation of Lord Baltimore who felt it politically expedient to choose a Protestant governor as a sign of good will toward the Puritans in England. He had arrived in Virginia from England in 1633, settling in Accomac County on Virginia's Eastern Shore. There he married Verlinda Graves Cotton and settled on an 1800-acre land grant. Thomas the Signer descended from William's son John, John's son Thomas, and Thomas's son David. After serving as governor with distinction for four years William Stone was rewarded in 1653 by the Lord Proprietor with a grant of 5,000 acres on Nanjemoy Creek in western Charles County. Stone named his land Poynton Manor in honor of a village in southeast Lancashire, England, allegedly the 16th century home of the progenitors of the southern Maryland Stones. [12]

Thomas Stone was born at Poynton Manor in 1743. At this time his father David held a rather small portion of about 400 acres in the far southeastern corner of the original tract. The David Stone plantation lay just west of Stone's Creek (now Mill Run) where it flows into the easternmost stretch of Avon Creek, which in turn flows into the northeastern corner of the broad, greater Nanjemoy Creek. Poynton Manor is about three miles from the Potomac River and six miles southwest of Port Tobacco. Thomas was the first child born to David Stone and his second wife Elizabeth Jenifer Stone. The Stone-Jenifer union produced five sons and three daughters who survived to adulthood. The five boys were successful in various ways and degrees. However, Thomas, John Hoskins and Michael Jenifer made outstanding contributions to their county, State and Nation. John Hoskins (1750-1804) (the

---

12 Harry Wright Newman, *The Stones of Poynton Manor*, Washington D.C., 1937, pp. 7-8. Hereinafter, *Newman*.

This ancient house allegedly stood on the site of Governor William Stone's home which was built about 1660 and burned about 1740. Most likely Thomas and the rest of David and Elizabeth Jenifer Stone's children were born here. It was owned by the Stones until about 1890 and survived until nearly mid-20th century. During much of

Colonel), commanded a company and later a battalion in the Maryland Line in several critical Revolutionary War battles. He survived the terrible Maryland Line losses in the Battle of Long Island only to be seriously wounded at Germantown, Pennsylvania more than a year later. He was Governor of Maryland 1794-1797. Michael Jenifer Stone (1747-1812), practiced law in southern Maryland, was a member of the First Congress of the United States, and became Chief Judge of Maryland's First Judicial District.

Not a great deal is known about Thomas Stone's boyhood. It is doubtful that David Stone's plantation afforded his rather large family any significant comforts or privileges. Perhaps the family name was the major asset at this time. David's oldest son, Samuel, by his first wife, eventually inherited his father's plantation, but not until 1773 when David died. About 1880 Richard Moncure Conway of Stafford County, Virginia, sent Virginia genealogist Horace Edwin Hayden some background on Thomas Stone's early life. Conway was a great grandson of Thomas and Margaret Stone. His grandmother was Margaret, the Stone's older daughter who married Virginian Dr. John Moncure Daniel at Habre de Venture December 15, 1793. Conway's Stone family history stated that

> . . . *by 15 years of age Thomas had acquired a good*
> *knowledge of the English language . . . He entered*
> *a private school of Mr. Blaizedell, a Scotchman,*
> *who taught about 10 miles from Poynton Manor . . .*
> *Here he was taught Greek and Latin.* [13]

According to Conway, Thomas Stone's father was a gentleman of fortune. But in spite of that Thomas had to borrow money to enable him to go to Annapolis to study law in the office of barrister Thomas Johnson, Jr. Conway may be credited with the story of Margaret Brown and her 1,000-pound dowry which helped the Stones buy Habre de Venture in 1770. Conway also told Hayden that,

> *his* [Stone's] *practice for a part of this time* [in
> Charles County] *was not so prosperous as it had*
> *been in Frederick nor was his farm productive, most*

---

13 Horace Edwin Hayden, *Virginia Genealogies,* Brown family portion Baltimore reprint 1979, pp. 175-176. (Hereinafter, *Va. Genealogies.)*

of it being quite thin land and needing cultivation. [14]

Thomas Stone's association with Thomas Johnson (also from southern Maryland) began a life-long friendship -- a student-mentor relationship that seemed built on complimentary rather than like personalities or characteristics. Certainly it did not hurt Stone's budding reputation and growing barrister status to be thought an intimate of Thomas Johnson, Esq., who in 1777 became Maryland's first non-Colonial Governor. About 1765 Stone finished his apprenticeship in Annapolis and passed the Maryland bar. During that year he was admitted to practice in Baltimore, Frederick and Prince George's Counties, the Mayor's Court at Annapolis, and in Charles County the next year. [15]

---

14   Ibid, p. 176.

15 Edward C. Papenfuse, Alan F. Day, David W. Jordan and Gregory A. Stiverson, *A Biographical Dictionary of the Maryland Legislature, 1635-1789, Vol. 2: I-Z.* Baltimore and London, 1985. (Hereinafter, *MHR Biographical Dictionary.*)

The Forensic Club
Shaping Thomas Stone's Law Education

Like a bright flash the mid-18th Century Forensic Club flourished in Annapolis. It succeeded for eight years (1759-1767) in spite of extremely rigid, narrow qualifications for membership. This club's records have left us with several interesting indications that young Stone traveled with many of the socially, politically and intellectually elite living in or near the provincial capital. His historic family connections backed him up to be sure as soon as he arrived and joined the Thomas Johnson law firm and began the demanding study leading to bar membership anywhere in Maryland.

The Forensic Club was by and for members of the area law practice community. Some of the most distinguished members in the 1760's were – William Paca, Samuel Chase and Thomas Stone. These three served and protected Maryland's interests during the deliberations of the Continental Congress. This of itself is a true measure of the significance of the club – that it could attract and hold such a group for several years. Other super achievers in Maryland bench and bar representation in the club – Thomas Harwood, Daniel Dulaney, Richard Tilghman, George Digges, Arthur and Stephen Bordley, Thomas Johnson and Judge Jeremiah T. Chase. When joining the club the new members agreed to making **no** frivolous motions or notions – and **no** indecent language or behavior. Those who violated these house rules were assessed a rather heavy fine of two shillings and sixpence.

And into this tightly structured elitist company stepped a 19-year old and still very green lawyer, Thomas Stone. He was proposed for membership at the gathering of March 2, 1763. He had to have been considered a fully trained and professional member of the bar – not yet out of his teens. Stone was accepted into full membership when he was first proposed.

Each club meeting (about one a month) began with a sumptuous banquet-type meal. Afterward, the heart of it all – serious debates selected earlier by club members. All had to participate and debate subjects were selected ahead of time and the debaters were told which side to take. What a truly marvelous "graduate school" experience this must have been for young Stone – doubtless about half the age of the older members.

After about a year and a half of regular attendance at club meetings Stone began to be absent rather frequently. On June 30, 1766 Stone was excused from paying his club expenses " . . . during his continuance out of town." He attended no meetings after April 7, 1766. This fact seems to indicate that Stone's new law practice in Frederick was placing ever increasing demands on his time and energy.

The influence of the debates on Stone's law education must have been great. After all, he was participating face-to-jowl with the most experienced lawyers to be found in the Annapolis area . . . many with decades of practice behind them. Debate subjects seemed always to be a somewhat conjectural case not easily resolved through English Common Law of provincial ordinances. Subjects of debate in which Stone took either the negative or affirmative:

- Whether civil society was introduced by consent?
- Whether a soldier doubting the justice of war ought to fight?
- Whether theft in any case is lawful?
- Whether sovereignty can be acquired by conquest?
- Whether the sea is free?

Stone's debating experience placed him often on the victorious team. As a courtroom trial lawyer Stone may have been quite successful. That type of action simply could not show Stone at his best – in the orderly, quiet world of written communication. [16]

---

16 George Forbes collection, *Record of Forensic Club Meetings and Membership, 1759-1767,* Maryland Hall of Records, Annapolis, MD, MSA SC4389, MS.

Early Law Practice

Study of Thomas Stone's law practice correspondence strongly indicates that for a short time he struggled to maintain a practice in Frederick, Port Tobacco and Annapolis. He was eligible to pursue his law affairs in his native county after 1766. Somewhat surprising is the date of a 1770 Port Tobacco letter from Stone to Mrs. Jeremiah Townley Chase in Annapolis. He advised this client that she should await the end of his planned "fortnight" in Frederick. At this time Stone had not yet even purchased the Habre de Venture land, which leads to a bit of a mystery – where were Thomas, Margaret and Frederick living at mid-summer 1770? Older daughter Margaret was born in 1770. Where? Stone's letter implies rather clearly that it was written at "Portobacco." [17]

Trying to keep up his professional business while handling clientele in three quite separated communities must have nearly drained Stone, physically and mentally. This young father of twenty-six years, with at least one child, probably spent much time away from home. Travel discomforts alone must have been brutal. Beginning about ten years later Stone's brothers mentioned in their correspondence their brother Thomas's bouts of ill health. Thomas himself alluded to his fragile health during the same period.

Stone must have done fairly well in Frederick. About 1768 he felt sure enough of his future to marry a long-time acquaintance, Miss Margaret Brown of Charles County. [18] She was the youngest daughter of the venerable and well-to-do Gustavus Brown, M.D., of Charles County. The Thomas Stones lived in Frederick probably three years. Perhaps drawing heavily on his wife's dowry, Stone purchased the Habre de Venture-Hanson's Plains Enlarged property near Port Tobacco from his uncle, Daniel Jenifer, a brother of Daniel of St. Thomas Jenifer. The Stones paid 400 pounds "sterling

---

17 Maryland Historical Society, Baltimore, Md., letter Thomas Stone to Mrs. Jeremiah Townley Chase, June 16, 1770, MS 1303.

18 *Biographical Dictionary, op.cit.*

of Great Britain" for 442 acres that had been surveyed for Jenifer in 1767. [19]

Even though great grandson R. M. Conway stated about 1880 that the Stones had difficult going in Charles County for a few years county land records indicate that during the five years they spent here before the outbreak of the Revolutionary War Thomas was very active in buying and selling local real estate. Records do not indicate exactly when Thomas and Margaret moved into their new plantation house at Habre de Venture. However, family records indicate the older daughter, Margaret, was born in Charles County in 1770, and Mildred, the younger, in 1772. One or both may have been born in one of two tenements standing at Habre de Venture in late 1767.

In the fall of 1773 the main dwelling house apparently was not quite complete since Stone was then ordering a considerable amount of white lead and doorsteps from merchant Robert Christie in Baltimore. [20] However, the gravestone of younger Stone daughter Mildred at Crow's Nest in Stafford County, Virginia, indicates clearly that she was born in Charles County February 27, 1772. This does not necessarily signify that the new house was completed by this date. And it does not prove Mildred was born in the new Habre de Venture mansion house.

Inscribed neatly but faintly on a brick near the northwest corner of the main north wall of the house are the words "Thos Stone Anno Domini 1773." Construction could not have started before the spring of 1771. Probably the Stones did not move into the new house until 1772, possibly before it was entirely finished. Frederick no doubt was born in Frederick, Maryland in 1769 while Thomas and Margaret lived there.

In 1773, while still working to improve his Habre de Venture property, and struggling to build his local law practice,

---

19 Archives of Maryland , Maryland Hall of Records, Annapolis, MD., Charles County Land Records, Liber S3, pp. 127-130. Hereinafter *C. C. Land Records.*

20 Myers collection #758, 1 and 2, Rare Books and Manuscripts Div., New York Public Library, NY, NY. Thomas Stone to Robert Christie, Jr., Baltimore, Sept. 17, 1773.

Stone jumped into politics as a member of the Charles County Committee of Correspondence, an early awareness of the need to address developing frictions with Great Britain.

In 1774 Stone was asked by Royal Governor Robert Eden to help prosecute a Maryland Legislator. Displaying much courage, Stone on the Governor's behalf took part in the suit involving a Royal Decree that bound all citizens of the Crown to pay a poll tax for support of the Anglican Church, the official Church of England since Henry VIII. The tax had long been bitterly resented and often resisted by non-members of the Anglican community in Maryland. His pro-Colony involvement in this case seems not to have tarnished Stone's increasing reputation as one of the State's up-and-coming young members of the bar. [21]

He also represented Charles County in the Provincial Conventions that governed Maryland from 1774 through 1776. From 1776 until his death Thomas Stone served in county, State, and national positions of increasing trust and responsibility, occasionally at two or all three levels at the same time. He was elected in December 1774 to serve as a Maryland delegate to the First Continental Congress. Then, he was elected in 1775, 1776 and 1777 to serve in the Second Continental Congress. Although elected again in February 1777, he did not attend sessions of Congress that year. He was elected again in December that year but did not attend sessions until 1778. He was elected to Congress the last time in November 1783 but did not attend until March 1784. Finally, in February 1787, Stone was elected by the Assembly to be a Maryland delegate to the Philadelphia Convention. But he decided not to serve, no doubt primarily because of his wife's precarious health. [22]

---

21   Dumas Malone, ed., *Dictionary of American Biography.* 9 vols. New York, 1936, 9:pp. 84, 85.

22   *Biographical Dictionary, op.cit.* Vol. 2, p. 788.

Thomas Stone
and the Maryland Council of Safety

Even while representing Maryland in the Continental
Congresses Stone returned frequently to Annapolis and participated
knowledgeably and energetically in the conduct of provincial
affairs. From early 1774 until 1777 the fortunes and misfortunes of
Maryland were managed with varying degrees of success by the
several Conventions sitting at Annapolis. Even though the
Provincial Convention members held very tight reins over their
delegates in Congress, they themselves initiated and encouraged
unstintingly actions that supported the other colonies in opposing
British oppression. This cooperation lined Maryland up rather
clearly in the arena of treason whether or not Convention members
saw it this way. While the Convention exhorted its delegates in
Congress to tread very lightly on matters of disassociation with the
Mother Country they themselves supported a Colony-wide trade
embargo against Britain and established an independent militia.
Both acts loudly proclaimed Maryland's intent to promote a united
all-colony front against British intransigence and attempts at
coercion. The Convention sitting in 1775 from July 26 until August
14 adopted resolutions that committed the province to continuing
both commercial and military resistance against Great Britain. It
voted to raise forty companies of militia, to print more than
266,000 pounds in bills of credit, and, perhaps most significantly, it
created a Council of Safety to handle the governmental affairs of
Maryland between meetings of the Convention which under the first
Constitution of Maryland, was known as the Maryland Assembly..

In effect, this Council became a stabilizing and continuing
arm for the Convention, with surprisingly broad governmental
authority. The major role of the Council was to do what had to be
done to "put Maryland in the best state of defense." Initially, the
Council was composed of sixteen members. It had complete
authority to supervise defense preparations and regulate Maryland's
military establishment. It could even order its militia in minute-man
type organizations to operate in other colonies. The following
Convention, which met in January 1776, made some significant
changes in the size of the Council and the nature of its
responsibilities, which endured until the need for the Council ended
in March 1777, when the new State government under the 1776

Constitution took over the responsibilities and functions of the Council of Safety. So, for more than a year, the Council existed as the most powerful single political entity in Maryland.

Thomas Stone, delegate to the Convention from Charles County, as well as delegate to the Continental Congress, was the primary architect of the reorganization of the 1777 Council of Safety. The original draft written by Stone proposing reorganization of the Council exists in the Maryland Hall of Records. Though undated and unsigned it has been identified positively as the work of Thomas Stone.

From May to July 1775 Stone had been in Philadelphia, but he returned to Annapolis later in the year to serve as Charles County delegate to the Convention. There he was a member of a committee responsible for preparing a plan of defense for the Colony. His committee also chartered the Council of Safety. He returned to the Continental Congress later in 1775 and then came back to Annapolis to participate in the Convention that began December 7. Both inter-colony and intra-colony affairs with respect to relationships with the mother country were fast reaching critical and dangerous conditions. The loyalist enemy within at this time seemed to threaten the total well-being of Maryland more than any external threat.

Very early in 1776 it seemed clear that the State needed a more effective, forceful Council of Safety to speak and act for the Convention quickly and decisively between meetings of the Convention. Thomas Stone's draft proposing reorganization of the Council was quickly approved by the Convention and a new charter adopted January 17. The existing draft bears alterations made by persons other than Stone, but they are of the most minor kind. Under the new charter the Council functioned in a more orderly manner, and kept its authority for overseeing Maryland's military forces and defense posture. Also, the Convention now allowed the Council to sit continuously, when necessary. And the new Council charter clearly gave it the right to pardon men sentenced to death by military tribunal -- a very great and significant power indeed. The pardoning power expressly called for in the Stone draft represented a major change from the charter of the first Council. Certainly Thomas Stone's experience in the Convention in connection with the reorganization of the Council of Safety gave this young lawyer from Port Tobacco a broad political, judicial, and even military expertise that increased his ability to serve his native Maryland extremely well as a member of Congress. [23]

As the fast- breaking events held the full attention of Congress during early 1776, Stone and his three Maryland delegate-companions probably chafed more than a little trying to live within the constraints placed upon them by the Convention. Keeping up with happenings in Congress and playing a very important contemporaneous role in his State's government must have been exhausting for Stone. Simply having to travel great distances under nearly unbearable road conditions had to be very taxing -- Annapolis to Philadelphia and return, Annapolis to Port Tobacco and return, or perhaps Port Tobacco all the way to Philadelphia and back home, countless times for several years. Stone for most of his adult life was not a robust, healthy person, which may have been part of the reason he seemed taciturn and not overly sociable to some of his peers. He was described by his contemporaries as being tall and slightly built, introspective and retiring. This somewhat delicate appearing, non-cosmopolitan type of country gentleman from southern Maryland between 1774 and 1787 undertook almost unbelievably complex, demanding, frustrating and controversial, often overlapping burdens in the public service. At the same time he nurtured an ever-growing law practice in Charles County and in Annapolis. For fifteen years he enjoyed ever increasing stature as a leading member of the Maryland Bar. While still only in his early thirties his county, state and nation called upon him frequently to assume always more demanding assignments in government.

Between 1771 and 1783 Thomas Stone struggled to keep a foot in the doors of both Charles County and Annapolis society and political matters. By early 1776 he had become acquainted with

---

23   Jean H. Vivian, "Thomas Stone and the Re-organization of the Maryland Council of Safety, 1776." *Maryland Historical Magazine,* Volume LXIX (1974), pp. 271-278. This article describes in a very well documented way how truly a significant historical figure Thomas Stone was in his native state even before he signed the Declaration of Independence. The author's research in support of her article is thoroughly substantive and scholarly and based on primary documentary evidence found in the Hall of Records, Annapolis, Maryland.

Charles Carroll, Barrister, one of the most distinguished and influential figures in the Maryland State Capital. A Stone note to Carroll of 1776 once used as a wrapper for other mail said,

> *Sir, I shall take the opportunity by a courier which will be sent from hence tomorrow, to transmit the letters to your son committed in my care, and shall at all times think myself happy in rendering you or him any service in my power. The last letters we received from him* [Archbishop John Carroll] *by Mr. Chase were from Montreal of the 13ᵗʰ of this month where they were. Mr. Franklin we hear is at Albany in a declining state. The post office is managed so very badly that no certain correspondence can be carried on through that channel. I am with most respectful comp. to the ladies.*
>
> *Yr most obt. Servt,*
> *T. Stone.* [24]

During most of his married life he was pressured by family problems that after 1776 included never ending remorse over his wife's continually failing health. About May 1776 his wife, Margaret, had been inoculated by the use of the mercurial treatment against small pox when she visited him in Philadelphia. Her entire system apparently was poisoned by the inoculation and she reacted in a very serious and increasingly painful way, suffering from arthritis in its most debilitating form. On top of this, Stone felt responsible for helping younger brothers and sisters in Charles County who for various reasons depended upon him for some of the most basic necessities and common comforts of life.

Even before his wife's lengthy illness began Stone found long periods of absence away from Habre de Venture very difficult. When sitting with the Fourth Convention in Annapolis in 1775, he wrote to Margaret at Habre de Venture:

> *We have this day received a confirmation of the unhappy contest* [at Lexington and Concord]

---

24 Maryland Historical Society, Baltimore, MD. Letter T. Stone to [Chas. Carroll of Annapolis], [May? 1776] used as a wrapper, MdHi, MS 206, No. 341 [692].

31

*between the King's troops and the people of New
England and I am afraid it is too true. This will
reduce both England and America to a state to
which no friend of either will ever wish to see; how
it will terminate, God only knows. My heart is with
you, and I wish it was in my power to see you, but
many gentlemen insist that I should stay to assist in
deliberation on those important affairs. I wish to
do my duty and shall be obliged to stay here
[Annapolis] longer than I expected, but I hope to
see you on Sunday, if nothing new occurs. We have
accounts that numbers of people are killed on both
sides; which I am apprehensive will preclude all
hopes of reconciliation between this and the Mother
Country . . . Pray God preserve you and bless our
little ones. We are like to see times which will
require all our fortitude to bear up against . . .* [25]

So, even early in 1775, more than a year before the
Declaration, Thomas Stone was preparing himself for what
appeared to be an almost inevitable split with the Crown. The
depth of his sacrifice in the cause of public service was
considerable. In 1775, at thirty-two years of age, Stone had to
leave a very young wife (now 24 years of age) and three small
children at Habre de Venture, an isolated plantation house, far from
the amenities of what society had to offer elsewhere in Maryland
during those years. Further, Stone's Charles County area law
practice needed every bit of attention he could give it. In 1775 he
probably had lived at Habre de Venture no more than three years
and was now participating in Charles County Bar matters with an
ever increasing commitment.

A few years later while Stone was a member of the
Maryland Senate one of his peers described him as

*a perfect man of business . . . he appeared to be
naturally of an irritable temper, yet he was mild
and courteous in his general deportment, fond of
society and conversation and universally a favorite*

---

25   J. Thomas Scharf, *A History of Maryland*, 3 Vols. Baltimore, 1879,
Vol. 2, pp. 2, 235. Hereinafter *Scharf.*

from his great good humor and intelligence . . .
There were few men who could commit their
thoughts to paper with more facility or greater
strength of argument. [26]

This picture of Stone does not portray him as an anti-social, drab character in the least.

Under the able stewardship of lawyer W. B. Stone Habre de Venture may well have presented such an attractive face about 1875. Photo John M. Wearmouth

26   *Ibid.*

Continental Congress Delegate

During early 1776 Stone's outlook toward ties with Britain shifted gradually as changing political events reshaped the attitude of many in Congress. On April 24, 1776, writing from Philadelphia, Thomas Stone told his uncle Daniel of St. Thomas Jenifer in Annapolis that

> *I wish to conduct affairs so that a just and honorable reconciliation should take place, or that we should be pretty unanimous in a resolution to fight it out for independence, the proper way to effect this is not to move too quick. But, then, we must take care to do everything which is necessary for our security and defense, not suffer ourselves to be lulled or wheedled by any deceptions, declarations, or givings out. You know my heart wishes for a peace upon terms of security and justice to America. But war, anything, is preferable to a surrender of our rights.* [27]

These are not the words of a man irresponsibly dead-set against separation from Britain, three months away from the Declaration of Independence. Rather, they reflect normal, respectable feelings of a rational, intelligent, patriotic statesman, fearing the worst but still clinging to hope for a reasonable settlement that would not jeopardize the honor, freedom, and safety of his fellow Americans.

Stone did not stand alone in such an outlook. His close friend Thomas Johnson continued to feel that the government of Great Britain was

> *. . . fundamentally beneficent; that the Colonies should ever hold in mind the prospects of reconciliation with the Crown.*

But he would be ready for war, if war seemed inevitable. In October 1775 Thomas Johnson had told Congress that,

> *. . . I see less and less prospect of a reconciliation*

---

27 Archives of the State of Maryland, Maryland Hall of Records. State Papers, Red Book 1, #25A - 25B. Letter Thomas Stone to Daniel of St. Thomas Jenifer (original).

every day . . .

And for the next seven months Thomas Stone stood with Johnson in this view of things. [28]

Stone's deep feelings and broad comprehension of issues related to dissolution of ties to Britain lay hidden for nearly 200 years. A letter written May 20, 1776 by him was featured in a 1957 Library of Congress publication article entitled "The Dye is Cast." This letter introduced historians to a Thomas Stone they never fully understood. It was composed by an astute statesman who had a learned and sensitive comprehension of those trying and uncertain times that many Colonials could not fully grasp. Some feared to face the facts entirely while others were injudiciously prepared to plunge into open warfare with the greatest naval power of the 18th century. Today this 1776 letter is our chief source of information about Thomas Stone's thinking during the crucial weeks immediately preceding the Declaration of Independence. Any broad, insightful comprehension of Stone's character and intellect must rest to considerable degree on this letter. It deserves extensive quoting. Historians feel the "Dear Sir," salutation is directed towards James Hollyday, an old friend of Thomas Stone from Talbot County, Maryland. He was a lawyer and had been a Maryland Assemblyman, Councilor, and member of several Maryland Provincial Conventions, 1774-76, as well as of the Council of Safety for the Eastern Shore. Excerpts from the letter are as follows

> *I am very much obliged by the intelligence*
> *communicated in yours of the 17th and much*
> *pleased by the temper shewn* [sic] *in the Convention*
> *[in Annapolis] -- tho I fear it can now be of little*
> *service in the general scale of American politics.*
> *The Dye is Cast.[29] The fatal stab is given to any*
> *future connection between this country and Britain:*
> *Except in the relation of conquorer* [sic] *&*
> *vanquished, which I can't think of without Horror*

---

28 Edward S. Delaplaine, *The Life of Thomas Johnson*. New York, 1927, p. 159.

29 This refers to the Continental Congress resolves of May 10 and 15 urging Provincial Assemblies and Conventions to establish governments adequate to secure "the happiness and safety of their constituents." These resolves were everything but an open declaration of independence and Hollyday had informed Thomas Stone about the Maryland Convention's reaction to the Congressional resolves. Maryland supported the resolves, a surprise to Stone who had not favored such action.

*and Indignation . . . But in whatever is determined
it will be wise and prudent to have the Concurrence
of the People. I wish much to be with you & to
remain with you to share in all your perplexities,
Difficulties & Dangers be they what they may. But
I am denied the only Comfort I could have in the
present Situation of affairs by the particular
Circumstances of my family. I am distressed
beyond the Bearing of a Man who has much more
Philosophy than ever I was blessed with, by
contemplating probable Events in this Country.
And this mortifying Speculation is not the greatest
uneasiness I suffer at present. The Illness of a wife
I esteem most dearly preys most severely on my
Spirits, she is I thank God something better this
afternoon, and this Intermission of her Disorder
affords me Time to write to you The doctor thinks
she is in a fair way of being well in a few days. I
wish I thought so. The People of this Province are
thrown into the most violent Convulsions by the
resolve of Congress sent you, the result of which it
is impossible to foresee . . . Our affairs in Canada
are ruined as you will see by the Papers. I wish we
may make a tolerable stand on any Ground the
other side of the Lake [Champlain]. I hear [Samuel]
Chase has wrote to a friend of his in this city, that
he could not be of any further service in Canada
and was determined to sit [set] out the day after he
wrote, to leave the Country, should this resolution
be taken by our Commissioners there, which
however I hope for their Credit & our Safety will
not be the Case. The Soldiers will probably follow
& will not even hazard a Stay at Saint Johns or the
Isle au Noix to raise fortifications, should this be
the case & the Enemy take the advantage of this
consternation and regain the Lakes, assemble the
Canadians who are very generally irritated against
us & the Indians who will join the Party to
appearance victorious, a most bloody & destructive
war upon the Frontiers of N York & N England will
ensue, and how far it's Consequences may extend,
cannot be foretold--on the contrary should a proper
Stand be made at St. Johns, the Isle au Noix
fortified & the Lake secured, which I have yet*

Hopes will be done, we may keep them at least this Campaign from penetrating the back Parts of the Country . . . All the Evil consequences which were seen and pointed out by men averse to this Canada Expedition will I fear be felt, and even then those who were for it will not ascribe them to the true Cause, the fundamental Error of the undertaking . . . The people of England talk much of Settlement with America . . . it is said 30 or 40 thousands Troops will be sent to America, 10000 for the South, 10000 for Canada, the rest for the Northern Provinces . . . I think it very probably [sic] *Commissioners will be sent with the Troops, tho I very much doubt of the Sincerity of administration to offer just & reasonable Terms to us. I do not form this opinion upon the Circumstance of Troops being sent for I think they will naturally suppose if Commissioners are sent without support we must dictate the Terms of Accomodation* [sic] *& they may also readily conceive they will not be of the most moderate kind. But I fear the Ministry* [of Great Britain] *are strongly attached to their Sistem,* [sic] *perhaps from Principle, that they have discovered the strong Inclination to Peace in many Colonies & are in hopes, by offering something like reasonable Terms at a Time when the Distresses of war are painted strongly upon the minds of those who have not been irritated & enraged by feeling them in reality, to create Divisions & Dissentions through the Country . . . should the most reasonable Terms be offered preserving the subordinate relation of this Country to Britain I much question if they would be accepted by the present haughty Temper of America . . . The difficulties respecting Governor* [Robert] *Eden's removal from or stay in Maryland which you mention occurred to me, but upon the whole I was of opinion it would be best to get him out of the Province in a peaceable Manner, if it could be done, because I thought it wrong in our present Circumstances to suffer a Correspondence to be carried on between any persons here & Administration the contents of which we were not acquainted with, And because I was apprehensive the Governor's unguarded Conduct whatever his*

*Intentions may be would frequently afford an
handle for designing Men to imbroil and inflame
the Province, and I did not see any Disadvantages
flowing from his Departure of so much consequence
of these, however if he pledges his Honour & Safety
not to correspond & conduct himself peaceably,
perhaps his Stay may be reconciled to every Body,
unless you should assume Government & appoint a
Governor of your own & in that case I suppose the
Ground must be given up entirely to the Master
elect. I wrote to the convention [of Maryland]
signifying my Inclination to be recalled from hence,
in which I was & am much in Earnest. My situation
is truly disagreeable--could I sit with the same
happy Indifference I observe in others when matters
of the last consequence are in agitation or could I
bring my mind to view with Apathy the destructive
Tendency of Measures or at least appearing to me
so, which I can't prevent, or could I bring my
Temper to bend to the Principles of those, who
perhaps are wiser than myself, I should be less
miserable. But my feelings are too keen, my
Concern for those whose happiness I wish to secure
too exquisite & my Constitution too stiff to allow of
my Continuance with tolerable Ease to myself.
These things however should not weigh with me if I
had any Prospect of my being serviceable: But I
should ill reward the confidence reposed in me by
the Convention if I was not to be explicit in my
Information to them that I was totally useless &
only served to give fruitless Opposition to Measures
which I can't approve but which however may be
right, as they are adopted by wiser men--And that
no Advantage derived from my Stay here was equal
to the Expence of my support, and this is in sober
Sadness my opinion, if they think proper to order
Deputies from there again to take a Seat in
Congress & under all these circumstances to
appoint me one I will most certainly serve them to
the best of my Judgment, as I am principled against
quitting any Post where my Countrymen think I may
be usefull however disagreeable it may be to myself
or whatever my own Opinion may be on the Subject
provided it be not against my Principles of*

*Morality, in which I will ever retain the absolute
Dominion . . . Let me hear from you & be assured I
am with most sincere Esteem, Yr constant friend &
obt. Servt.,*

T. Stone

Monday night

*I have missed the Post by attending to hear the
Intelligence above referred to. I must now send
this by Mr. [Robert] Alexander* [30] *who will give
you a particular account thereof. It is bad
enough, & will be published. There are Treaties
for foreign Troops to the amount I think of near
20000. Several Letters say we have nothing to
rely on but our own Strength. The People of
England [are] uneasy, & the American Cause
gains Ground--One letter mentions
Commissioners--no names to any. The whole
Number of Troops intended for America, 34000--
this number tho it may appear large will I am
hopefull & indeed convinced will not be adequate
to the diabolical Purpose of Conquest for which
they are designed . . . What Part France will take
is not known but it is most probable she will be
influenced by the same vile motives with the other
European Powers. If our councils Could but be
tempered with a proper Degree of moderation &
attention to the Inclinations & even weaknesses of
our people all would be well; but I think they will
not drive & an Attempt to do such an injury to the
feelings of freemen will have fatal Consequences.
May God attend your Deliberations & Direct them
to the right way. We are anxious to hear
something from you . . . My wife is something*

---

30   This Robert Alexander was another Maryland delegate to the Congress.
In late 1777 he defected from the Revolutionary cause and joined the British
as civil advisor in Philadelphia. He was later convicted of treason in absentia
but fled to England after the American victory.

better this morning & I hope will do well:[31] *Adieu*
my friend, remember me to all who you know I
think worth being remembered by. Yrs, T S [32]

It was only three weeks later that Virginia's Richard Henry
Lee read his resounding resolution that

These United Colonies are, and of right ought to be,
free and independent states.

And now a committee was formed to draft the formal Declaration
of Independence. Stone had seen the whole thing in sharp, logical
perspective, including the fact that the resolutions of May 10 and
15 calling for the colonies to form new independent governments
were indeed firm, irreversible acts of total rebellion. Finally, on
June 28, Maryland's Provincial Convention authorized its delegates
in Philadelphia to support Congressional acts that would lead to
separation from Great Britain. So, even the Provincial government
officials in Annapolis, well insulated from the heat of the trials and
pressures in Philadelphia, now felt as did Thomas Stone that the
Dye is Cast.

Thomas Stone's letter of May 20 to his friend Hollyday
revealed that the Maryland delegate from Charles County had a
wide, profound understanding of many issues, events, and
conditions that concerned the Continental Congress at this time.
He was, of course, deeply agitated over the prospect of Britain
sending thousands of troops, foreign and domestic, to enforce royal
laws, policies, and decrees that had rankled the Colonials for well
over a decade.

It became obvious to Stone by late May 1776 that the
British government (called the Ministry by Stone) did not intend to
negotiate or compromise with their upstart, recalcitrant Colonials.
If 40000 troops were required to beat them into submission, well,
so be it. At this time Thomas Stone could see no alternative to war
as much as he dreaded to the greatest depths of his being the
prospect of such a course. We can be quite certain now that when
Thomas Stone approved the Declaration of Independence on the
2nd of July, he did so fearfully, perhaps, but resolutely and with few

---

31   It seems clear that at this time Margaret was visiting Thomas in
Philadelphia and had recently been given mercurial inoculation against small
pox. This event brought much grief and discomfort to Margaret during the
rest of her short life

32   D.S. & V.L.Eaton, "The Dye is Cast," *The Library of Congress Quarterly
Journal of Current Acquisitions*, Vol. 14, nr. 4 (Aug. 1957), pp. 181-185.
Hereinafter *The Dye is Cast.*

reservations.

> *Reconciliation . . . like an agreeable dream,*
> *has passed away and left us . . .*

wrote the perceptive Thomas Paine in January 1776. Early in the
year this conclusion became obvious to most of the delegates in
Philadelphia. It is surprising that it took until July for Congress to
shape and articulate a united stand against Great Britain, which
indeed recognized that reconciliation no longer was even a
consideration. [33]

An interesting sidelight on these times and events appeared
in the *National Journal,* February 28, 1826, allegedly in the words
of Chief Justice Roger Brooke Taney (eulogizing Thomas Johnson)

> *When the Declaration of Independence was to be*
> *signed, after its adoption, Samuel Chase, then a*
> *young lawyer and dependent upon his profession*
> *for a living, went to Charles Carroll and asked his*
> *opinion. He promptly answered, "We should sign."*
> *He got a similar answer from* [William] *Paca.*
> *Then, going to Thomas Stone he said, "Stone, we*
> *need not hesitate. If Carroll and Paca are willing*
> *to risk their large estates with their necks, we who*
> *have nothing but our necks to lose may surely risk*
> *the halter." [34]*

Stone's concern over conditions in Canada was based on
the utter and costly failure of the audacious but ill-conceived two-
pronged American assault on Quebec in late 1775. The
expedition's commander, Brigadier General Richard Montgomery,
died there in December in early fighting just outside the southwest
approaches to the City of Quebec. Colonel Benedict Arnold
(commander of the New England troops marching through Maine
along the Kennebec and Chaudiere Rivers--incredible suffering all
the way to Quebec--cold, starvation, hostile terrain, poor
equipment) was wounded near the north city wall and Virginia's
Captain Daniel Morgan was taken prisoner there late in December.
The very few, ill, poorly clothed and supplied, demoralized
Colonials straggled homeward during most of 1776. They had
remained near Quebec City until British reinforcements arrived in
May. By late July the entire American force had reached the
southern end of Lake Champlain. They could not defend

---

33   Lillian B. Miller, *The Dye is Now Cast, The Road to American
Independence 1774-1776.* Washington, D. C., 1975. P. 234.

34   *National Journal,* February 28, 1826.

themselves against any organized Canadian attack at this point let alone protect the far western outposts of New York and New England. Stone was aware of these things--he knew how antagonized the Canadians were over the American assault, and in May and June 1776 he feared reprisals and even invasion at any time. Fortunately, the threat was not realized on any grand scale until mid-1777 when Major General John Burgoyne with crack British regulars, professional German mercenaries, and uncontrollable Iroquois allies, struck deeply into New York State before being stopped in the Battle of Saratoga, September-October 1777, only 25 miles north of Albany. [35]

Stone, during 1775 and 1776, was deeply involved in matters of military concern about Maryland's contribution to the Continental Congress' war effort. And, he worried much about Royal Navy depredations along the Potomac, threatening his own Charles County.

Hardly had independence been declared before Congress realized that the now "free and independent" States of North America were quite without a rudder, being bound together primarily through a mutual interest in dealing effectively with the military might of Great Britain, then broadly recognized as one of the most formidable powers in the world. The Continental Congress in 1776 had pathetically little authority to raise troops, tax, provide armament, or even procure basic provisions for the growing American military establishment. A few wise and prudent men in most of the Colonies now saw an obvious desperate need for a centralized government that would have at least enough consolidated power to conduct the war. Unfortunately, many heads not so wise, cool or unselfish, could not yet accept a political authority superimposed on the thirteen individual colonial governments. Regardless of such feelings, however, efforts were launched formally by Congress at mid-1776 to draft what came to be known as Articles of Confederation.

---

35   Lynn Montross, *Rag, Tag and Bobtail.* New York, 1952. PP. 65-70, 113, 209-225.

The Adams Papers (John) disclose some interesting observations about the machinations of the Continental Congresses. Some of the delegates may have felt New Englanders as a group were unreasonable in their passion to sever ties with Britain as soon as possible. However, until 1780 the southern colonies had not suffered any major incursions by British military might. New England on the other hand had been war-baptized at the Boston Massacre, Lexington-Concord, Bunker Hill and the Montgomery-Arnold epic and tragic assault on Quebec late in 1775. So, of course people like Samuel, John and Abigail Adams had lived within shouting distance of armed rebellion pain for nearly two years before the Declaration of Independence. For months delegates from southern colonies did not energetically support the New England early and all-out break with the Crown. Some of these views show in John Adams' comments in his letters through about 1780.

The Adams diary for September 8, 1775 describes a visit by John and Samuel Adams to a couple of "Maryland Gentlemen," Messrs. Paca and Chase in Philadelphia. Adams thought Chase

> . . . *ever social and talkative . . . his Colony*
> [Maryland] *have acted with Spirit in Support of the*
> *Cause.* [36]

From these words we may assume that the radical Massachusetts fire-brands were satisfied with Maryland's attitude toward independence. Adams would meet Thomas Stone in October 1775 when the youngest Maryland delegate took his seat in the Second Continental Congress.

One of Stone's first challenges in Congress concerned a proposal to do away with the King's Post -- long a critical Colonial communication mail link, and replace it with a "Constitutional Post" already established along the east coast. In the debate on this matter Stone (October 1775) asked for postponing a vote -- in part because he felt the new mail system in de facto had "already put down the old one." And about this time Stone took active part in arguing the pros and cons of the non-export policy in effect. One Colony, South Carolina, wanted an exemption to allow her to trade produce to those who had gun powder to sell the Colonies. In this

---

36 *John Adams Diary and Autobiography*, L. H. Butterfield, Editor, Vol. 2, Diary 1771-1781, Cambridge, Mass. P. 176.

month Stone in a show of independent thinking opposed fellow Delegate Chase in the deliberations about free trade -- Stone supported limited exporting -- otherwise the hamstrung Colonial Export policies

> . . . *appear to be a destructive system.*

He calls the Restraining Bill (to severely reduce exporting)

> *a most cruel, unjust, unconstitutional Act*

which would place all Americans . . .

> *in the same circumstances of poverty and distress.*

In July 1776, when printers' ink was still wet on copies of the Declaration of Independence, a small elite group of delegates was instructed by the Congress to develop the framework of a new central political authority to speak and act with one voice for the thirteen Colonies. During early discussions the smaller States expressed their deep concern over the western lands given several large colonies in original charters from the King. This stumbling block would stymie ratification of the new Articles of Confederation for five years. Stone was appointed a member of the new central government committee in July 1776 and signed the initial draft. The painful inadequacies of our first national authority doubtless disturbed Thomas Stone until his death. While he wasn't physically present at the 1787 Constitutional Convention, his earlier efforts to create a strong and workable central governing authority were marked by the Convention stepping stones leading to Philadelphia from Mount Vernon. [37]

Adams' August 2, 1776 notes detail the acrimonious debates over management of the western lands, which many claimed extended to the "South Sea" (Pacific Ocean). The smaller Colonies felt that the large Colonies eventually would gain population and size that would in effect cancel the true benefits of a republican, democratic government in which each State was guaranteed an equitable voice in any central government structure to be devised. The Maryland delegates championed the cause of those small States not able to claim westward extensions of their Atlantic Coast real estate: Initially, they were Maryland, Delaware, New Jersey, Connecticut and Rhode Island. [38]

Referring to this western lands threat to those who had no property west of the States that then existed, Thomas Stone spoke

---

37 *Journals of the Continental Congress.* National Archives and Records Service, Washington, D.C. Hereinafter *Journals.*

38 *Ibid.*

on August 2, 1776 --

> *This argument is taken up upon very wrong ground.*
> *It is considered as if we were voting away the*
> *territory of particular Colonies, and gentlemen*
> *work themselves up into warmth, upon that*
> *supposition. . . The small Colonies have a right to*
> *happiness and security. They would have no safety*
> *if the great Colonies were not limited. We shall*
> *grant lands in small quantities, without rent, or*
> *tribute, or purchase money. It is said that Virginia*
> *is attacked from every side. Is it meant that*
> *Virginia shall sell her western lands for its own*
> *emolument?*

Stone completed his comments with

> *. . .* ***all*** *the Colonies have defended these lands vs*
> *the King of Great Britain, and at the expense of*
> *all. . .?* [39]

ELEVATION of the .... STATE HOUSE

Familiar hallowed
walls for several
months to the
Signers from the
Thirteen Colonies.

---

39 *Ibid.*

The Signing

J. Thomas Scharf's milestone Maryland history published in 1879 relates in well researched scholarly detail the complexities facing Maryland delegates in the 2nd Continental Congress. [40] Since *Thomas Stone: Elusive Patriot* is primarily about the life of a Maryland Signer some details about the act of signing should be in order.

As summer of 1776 approached several Colonies had decided to support an early, complete break with England. It appeared to most of the Philadelphia delegates that the Colonies had gone that last mile toward appeasement. In Maryland, however, there existed pockets of doubt and fear about all out rebellion. Financial well being for many Maryland planters and business houses depended upon unbroken normal business relations with traditional banking houses and merchants in many centers of commerce all over the British Isles. Scharf's work outlines the strenuous efforts by Maryland's delegates, including Thomas Stone, to congeal State-wide support for the fast breaking impetus in Philadelphia toward early and complete rupture of American ties to Britain.

The machinery was set in motion shortly before the 15th of May. North Carolina had authorized her delegates to concur with the delegates from the other colonies "in declaring independency." Rhode Island had directed hers "to join in any measure to secure American rights." In Massachusetts, various towns had pledged themselves to maintain any declaration on which Congress might agree; and Virginia had given positive instruction for her delegates to propose that Congress should make a declaration of independence. [41] Then, on the 7th of June, Richard Henry Lee, on behalf of his colleagues, submitted a resolution declaring,

> . . . *that the United Colonies are and ought to be*
> *free and independent States; that they are absolved*

---

40   *Scharf, op.cit.*

41   Richard Frothingham, *The Rise of the Republic of the United States*, Tenth Edition. Boston, 1910. P. 512. Hereinafter *The Rise of the Republic.*

These fiery electric words by Richard Henry Lee lit the fuse and demolished all doubt as to the wisdom of the immediate separation.

Resolved ~~that~~

That these United Colonies are, and of right ought to be, free and independent States, that they are absolved from all allegiance to the British Crown, and that all political connection between them and the State of Great Britain is, and ought to be, totally dissolved.

That it is expedient forthwith to take the most effectual measures for forming foreign alliances.

That a plan of confederation be prepared and transmitted to the respective Colonies for their consideration and approbation.

from all allegiance to the British crown; and that
all political connection between them and the State
of Great Britain is, and ought to be, totally
dissolved.

This resolution was debated until the 10th of June, when it was postponed for three weeks so that the delegates who were instructed to oppose the measure could consult their constituents. These delegates included all those speaking for Maryland. Congress now requested each colony to express its sentiments on independence. Matthew Tilghman, Thomas Stone and Colonel John Rogers, on the 11th of June, wrote to the Maryland Council of Safety for instructions saying

The proposition from the delegates of Virginia, to
declare the colonies independent, was, yesterday,
after much debate, postponed for three weeks, then
to be resumed, and a committee is appointed to
draw up a declaration to prevent loss of time, in
case the congress should agree to the proposition at
the day fixed for resuming it. This postponement
was made to give an opportunity to the delegates
from those colonies which had not as yet given
authority to adopt this decisive measure, to consult
their constituents. It will be necessary that the
Convention of Maryland should meet as soon as
possible, to give the explicit sense of the province
on this point and we hope you will accordingly
exercise your power of convening them at such time
as you think the members can be brought together.
We wish to have the fair and uninfluenced sense of
the people we have the honor to represent, in this
most important and interesting affair, and it would
be well if the delegates to convention were desired
to endeavor to collect the opinion of the people at
large, in some manner or other, previous to the
meeting of convention. We shall attend the
convention whenever it meets, if it is thought proper
we should do so. The approaching harvest will,
perhaps, render it very inconvenient to many
gentlemen to attend the convention. This, however,

must not be regarded when matters of such
momentous concern demand their deliberation . . .
We see with the deepest concern the attempts from
various quarters to throw the province into a state
of confusion, division and disorder; but trust the
exertions of those who are the true friends of virtue
and the American cause, will be adequate to the
surrounding difficulties and dangers. From every
account and appearance, the king and his ministers
seem determined to hazard everything upon the
success of the sword, without offering any terms to
America which she ought to accept. That peace and
security which every virtuous man in the country
has so earnestly desired, seems not attainable in the
present disposition of the ruling powers of Britain
. . . The question for postponing the Declaration of
Independence was carried by seven colonies against
five. [42]

On the 14th of June, the Council of Safety, responded to that letter.

The Maryland Convention met at Annapolis June 21st with Matthew Tilghman as president, and immediately adopted the following resolution

> *Resolved, That the president of the*
> *convention inform the deputies of this province in*
> *congress, that their attendance in convention is*
> *desired; and that they move congress for permission*
> *to attend here; but that they do not leave the*
> *congress without such permission, and without first*
> *having obtained an order that the consideration of*
> *the questions of independence, foreign alliance, and*
> *a further confederation of the colonies shall be*
> *postponed until the deputies from this province can*
> *attend congress, which shall be as soon as possible.*

At the opening of the emergency session of the Convention there were present four members of Congress: Messrs. M. Tilghman, Samuel Chase, Robert Goldsborough and Thomas

---

42 *American Archives*, 4th series, vi, p. 807.

Johnson. Robert Alexander, Thomas Stone, William Paca and John Rogers were absent. Whether the absent members attended in accordance with the resolution adopted by the convention is not known. There was no mention of them in the proceedings of the convention. It is known that Mr. Paca remained in Philadelphia.

In the meantime, the Council of Safety, in accordance with the wishes of the members of Congress, had requested the county committees to call the freemen together to express their sentiments on the question of independence, and before the convention met the popular Colony-wide movement in its favor was evident in all the counties. Matthew Tilghman, Thomas Johnson and Samuel Chase left Congress to participate in the canvass and rouse the people to instruct their delegates in Convention to remove the restrictions which the Convention had put on them. The popular leaders who are found earliest identified with independence in the province are Samuel Chase, William Paca, Thomas Johnson, Matthew Tilghman, Charles Carroll of Carrollton, Charles Carroll, barrister, John Rogers, Thomas Stone, Turbutt Wright, James Hollyday, George Plater, Jeremiah T. Chase and Baker Johnson. In May and the early part of June, the people in county meetings renounced the hope of reconciliation and instructed their delegates to move for independence.

The freemen of Charles County, in their instructions to Josias Hawkins, Thomas Stone, Robert T. Hooe, Joseph H. Harrison and William Harrison, their delegates in convention, say

> *Reasons for the mode of voting and determining*
> *questions by a majority of counties, have not*
> *appeared to us to exist since the last general*
> *election; therefore we charge and instruct you to*
> *move for, and endeavor to obtain a regulation for*
> *voting individually, and determining questions by a*
> *majority of members, and not of counties, in future.*
> *And as we know we have a right to hear, or be*
> *informed, what is transacted in convention, we*
> *instruct you to move for, and endeavor to obtain, a*
> *resolve for the doors of the House to be kept open*
> *in future, and that on all questions proposed and*
> *seconded, the yeas and nays be taken, and together*
> *with every other part of your proceedings,*

50

*published, except such only as may relate to
military operations; questions which ought to be
debated with the doors shut, and the determinations
thereon kept secret.*

*The experience we have had of the cruelty and
injustice of the British government under which we
have too long borne oppression and wrongs, and
notwithstanding every peaceable endeavor of the
united colonies to get redress of grievances, by
decent, dutiful, and sincere petitions and
representations of the King and Parliament, giving
every assurance of our affection and loyalty, and
praying for no more than peace, liberty and safety
under the British government, yet have we received
nothing but an increase of insult and injury, by all
the colonies being declared in actual rebellion;
savages hired to take up arms against their lawful
masters; our towns plundered, burnt, and
destroyed; our vessels and property seized on the
seas, made free plunder to the captors, and our
seamen forced to take arms against ourselves; our
friends and countrymen, when captivated, confined
in dungeons, and, as if criminals, chained down to
the earth; our estates confiscated and our men,
women and children robbed and murdered; and as
at this time, instead of commissioners to negotiate a
peace, as we have been led to believe were coming
out, a formidable fleet of British ships, with a
numerous army of foreign soldiers, in British pay,
are daily expected on our coast to force us to yield
the property we have honestly acquired and fairly
own, and drudge out the remainder of our days in
misery and wretchedness, leaving us nothing better
to bequeath to posterity than poverty and slavery;
we must for these reasons declare that our affection
for the people and allegiance to the Crown of Great
Britain, so readily and truly acknowledge till of
late, is forfeited on their part. And as we are
convinced that nothing virtuous, humane, generous*

or just, can be expected from the British King or
nation, and that they will exert themselves to reduce
us to a state of slavery by every effort and artifice
in their power, we are of opinion that the time has
fully arrived for the colonies to adopt the last
measure for our common good and safety, and that
the sooner they declare themselves separate from,
and independent of the Crown and Parliament of
Great Britain, the sooner they will be able to make
effectual opposition, and establish their liberties on
a firm and permanent basis. We, therefore, most
earnestly instruct and charge you to move for,
without loss of time, and endeavor to obtain positive
instructions from the Convention of Maryland to
their delegates in Congress, immediately to join the
other colonies in declaring that the United Colonies
no longer own allegiance to, nor are they dependent
upon the Crown or Parliament of Great Britain, or
any other power on earth, but are, for time to come,
free and independent States; provided that the
power of framing government, and regulating the
internal concerns of each colony be left to their
respective Legislatures; and that the said delegates
give the assent of this province to any further
confederation of the Colonies for the support of
their union, and for forming such foreign
commercial connections as may be requisite and
necessary for our common good and safety. And as
the present government under the King cannot
longer exist with safety to the freemen of this
Province, we are of opinion a new form of
government, agreeable to the late recommendation
of the honorable Continental Congress to all the
United Colonies, ought immediately to be adopted.

This extraordinarily constructed document beautifully and forcefully
sets forth the attitudes and passions of Marylanders in general as
they embraced the cause of independence.

In view of the instructions from the counties and the stirring
appeals made through the press, the moderate members of the

convention, led by Chase, Carroll, Johnson and Tilghman, whose
influence was all powerful, gradually gave way to the popular will,
on the 14th of June. (Note that Stone was not included in this
group of moderates.) In previous Conventions they had
strenuously, but in vain, opposed the instructions which the
Convention of Maryland gave their representatives in Congress

> *to disavow, in the most solemn manner, all design*
> *in the colonies of independence.*

Chase was mortified in seeing himself and his colleagues in
Philadelphia tied down by those instructions. He took his seat in
the emergency special Convention after appealing to his
countrymen to make one more effort for their repeal and thereby
make it possible for Maryland delegates to follow the route to
complete separation. The question was immediately raised for
withdrawing the obnoxious instructions, and substituting the words

> *to concur with the other United Colonies, or a*
> *majority of them, in declaring the United Colonies*
> *free and independent States.*

Maryland delegates already had nearly arrived at the resolution to
proclaim independence. They feared that loss of a day might
deprive Maryland of a share in the glorious act about to take place.
Chase, Carroll, and their friends in the Maryland Convention,
brought all their energy, eloquence and arguments to bear in favor
of immediate action. On the 28th of June, the restrictive
instructions were repealed by the following resolution which was
substituted by Charles Carroll, of Carrollton

> *Resolved, unanimously, That the instruction*
> *given by the* [Maryland] *Convention of December*
> *last (and renewed by the Convention in May) to the*
> *deputies of this colony in Congress, be recalled,*
> *and the restrictions therein contained removed; that*
> *the deputies of this colony attending in Congress, or*
> *a majority of them,* **or any three or more of them,**
> *be authorized and empowered to concur with the*
> *other United Colonies, or a majority of them, in*
> *declaring the United Colonies free and independent*
> *States, in forming such further compact and*
> *confederation between them, in making foreign*
> *alliances, and in adopting such other measures as*

shall be adjudged necessary for securing the
liberties of America; and this colony will hold itself
bound by the resolutions of a majority of the
United Colonies in the premises: provided, the sole
and exclusive right of regulating the internal
government and police of this colony be reserved
to the people thereof.

How forceful and clear were these priceless words that gave Stone
and his fellow delegates the authority they desperately needed to
freely support the major thrust of Congress toward independence.

This turn-about by the Convention was hailed with lively
enthusiasm in all sections of the Colony and country. Congress
assembled on the 1st of July, in Independence Hall, Philadelphia,
and after the preliminary business was disposed of, the new
instructions were received by the Maryland delegates and read to
everyone's satisfaction. [43]

While Congress was considering the draft of a Declaration
of Independence, or the form of announcing the fact to the world,
the Maryland Convention, on the 3d of July, 1776, before they had
heard from Congress, adopted a declaration of their own in which
the grievances of the colonies were clearly set forth, and the
unalterable resolution of the people of Maryland was announced, to
maintain the common freedom of themselves and their posterity.

On the 2d day of July, after disposing of the business of the
morning, Congress resumed the consideration of the resolution of

---

43 *American Archives,* 4th series., p. 1194. John Adams, in a letter to Samuel
Chase dated Philadelphia, July 1, 1776, says: "Your favor by the post this
morning gave me much pleasure, but the generous and unanimous vote of your
convention gave me much more. It was brought into congress this morning just
as we were entering on the great debate; that debate took up most of the day,
but it was an idle mispense of time, for nothing was said but what had been
repeated and hackneyed in that room before a hundred times for six months
past. In the committee of the whole [Congress], the question was carried in the
affirmative, and repeated to the House. A colony desired it to be postponed
until tomorrow, when it will pass by a great majority, perhaps with almost
unanimity; yet I cannot promise this, because one or two gentlemen may
possibly be found who will vote point blank against the known and declared
sense of their constituents. Maryland, however, I have the pleasure to inform
you, behaved well; Paca, generously and nobly."

independence and finally agreed to the following

*Resolved, That these United Colonies are,
and of right, ought to be, free and independent
States; that they are absolved from all allegiance to
the British Crown, and that all political connexion
between them and the State of Great Britain, is, and
ought to be, totally dissolved.* [44]

Congress went immediately into a committee of the whole, with Benjamin Harrison of Virginia in the chair. During the remainder of that day, and during the sessions of July third and fourth, the phraseology, allegations and principles of the proposed declaration received close study. On the evening of the fourth, the committee rose and the chair reported the declaration as having been agreed upon. **It was then adopted by twelve States -- William Paca, John Rogers and Thomas Stone, casting the vote of Maryland.** None of these gentlemen deserved ever to be known as a "reluctant" Signer. All were bold, sensitive patriots in every way.

Congress ordered that the declaration be sent immediately to the several Colony Assemblies, Conventions and Committees or Councils of Safety, and to the several commanding officers of the continental troops. It went forth authenticated by John Hancock, president, and Charles Thomson, Secretary to the Congress. John Hancock, in transmitting a copy to the Maryland Convention, said

Philadelphia, July 8th, 1776.
*Gentlemen: -- Although it is not possible to
foresee the consequences of human actions, yet it is,
nevertheless a duty we owe ourselves and posterity,
in all our public comments, to decide in the best
manner we are able, and to trust the event to that
Being, who controls both causes and events so as to
bring about his own determination. Impressed with
this sentiment, and at the same time fully convinced*

---

44 *Journals, op.cit.*

The Signing, Philadelphia, July 4, 1776, *The Dye is Now Cast*, the Road to American Independence, National Portrait Gallery, Smithsonian Institution Press, the Historian's Office, Washington, 1975.

that our affairs may take a more favorable turn, the
congress have judged it necessary to dissolve all
connexion [sic] *between Great Britain and the*
American Colonies, and to declare them free and
independent States, as you will perceive by the
enclosed declaration, which I am directed by
congress to transmit to you, and to request you will
have it proclaimed in your colony in the way you
shall think most proper.

The important consequences to the
American States from this Declaration of
Independence, considered as the ground and
foundation of a future government, will naturally
suggest the propriety of proclaiming it in such a
manner as that the people may be universally
informed of it.

I have the honor to be, gentlemen,
Your most ob't humble
servant,
JOHN HANCOCK,
President.

And so there it was -- now presented to the freemen of Maryland.

The Maryland convention having adjourned, the Council of Safety sent copies to the Committee of Observation in all the counties, with the request that it should be proclaimed in the manner they might "judge most proper for the information of the people." It was printed in the *Maryland Gazette* of July 11th, and later it was proclaimed at the court house in Baltimore, in the presence of the independent companies and militia, amid loud applause, accompanied with salvos of artillery and "universal acclamations for the prosperity of the free United States." At night, the town was illuminated, and an effigy of the King of Great Britain paraded through the streets and burned in derision of his forfeited authority. It was received in a similar manner in other parts of the State.

In the records of the Maryland Land Office, in the handwriting of William Paca, is the following receipt, which shows who were the *three required* representatives of Maryland present in Congress between the 1st and 4th of July, 1776, when the

Declaration of Independence was adopted: They were William Paca, John Rogers and Thomas Stone. They all served America and Maryland extremely well and remain to this day brilliant stars in the Colonial history closure.

After three days of "fine tuning" Thomas Jefferson's masterful prose the final wording was adopted on the 4th of July. At this point it simply met the approval of the delegates present. It was not signed and probably was no more than several pages of ordinary long-hand script with final editorial changes still visible. For many years most Americans thought the final inspiring arty document developed full-blown and neatly signed on July 4th. Far from it! Many days passed before an "engrossed," impressive signed work was revealed to the public; the version Americans have known well for generations.

Not until July 19 was a resolution passed in Congress calling for the declaration approved on the 4th to be

> *fairly engrossed on parchment, with the title and*
> *style of The Unanimous Declaration of the Thirteen*
> *United States of America and then when engrossed*
> *it was to be signed by every member of Congress.*

According to Charles Thomson's *Journals of Congress* on August 2, 1776 the final beautiful parchment document was completed when signed by delegates from the thirteen former colonies of Great Britain.

The engrossing of the Declaration of Independence meant simply that it was to become an artfully contrived work done in generous dimension by calligraphers and artists specializing in creating written works that were often seen in prize specimens of poster-display artwork. Sometimes it was as impressive as many of the illuminated pages of medieval monastery books created by monks during several of the dark-age centuries . . . not at all out of order for such a priceless document as the Declaration of Independence of the United States of America.

The credentials of Matthew Tilghman, Thomas Johnson, Jr., William Paca, Samuel Chase, Thomas Stone, Charles Carroll of Carrollton, and Robert Alexander, the new members, who had been appointed by the Maryland Convention on the 4th of July, having been received by Congress on the 18th, that day appeared and took their seats. And, on the 2d of August, when the engrossed copy

Maryland's Four Signers with Thomas Jefferson.
Stanislav Rembski, Baltimore artist, is the painter
of this 1976 rendition. Standing (left to right)
William Paca, Thomas Jefferson and Thomas
Stone; (seated) Charles Carroll of Carrollton
and Samuel Chase.

Courtesy Mrs. Stanislav Rembski.

was laid on the desk of Secretary Thomson to be signed by the members **then present**. Samuel Chase, William Paca, Thomas Stone and Charles Carroll of Carrollton, affixed their names, thereby becoming indelibly etched in the illustrious history that marked the close of the American Colonial Period, to the everlasting distress and chagrin of the British Crown and Ministry. [45]

So, it was somewhat by happenstance that the delegate from Charles County became one of his State's four signatories, thereby gaining elevation to one of his Nation's loftiest places of honor and national recognition in perpetuity.

Any study of the exciting events leading to and immediately following the signing of the Declaration must lead to a deep respect for the courage and patriotism of those who signed. They gambled on a future shrouded in mists of uncertainty and shaky promises. Their risks are not diminished because all turned out well and the Signers as a group lived, kept their heads, and realized the ageless spectacular consequences of that simple act -- a signature on a piece of parchment.

Probably the patriots who achieved independence in North America gave little thought during their perilous trials to what a successful revolution against absolutist monarchy rule would signify elsewhere. The oppressed peoples of Europe had a fair understanding about American efforts to shake off Crown controls forever. And many in Europe (and in Latin America) doubtless felt the thirteen Colonies stood less than a ghost of a chance of staging a victorious revolution against a nation that was held even in Europe to be an almost invincible military and economic

---

45   It is stated that, as the signing was progressing, John Hancock, the President of Congress, asked Mr. Carroll, who had not the happiness of voting for the Declaration, if he would sign it? "Most willingly," he replied; and taking a pen, he signed his name, as was his habit, *Charles Carroll.* A bystander remarked aloud, as Mr. Carroll was signing his name, "There go several millions," alluding to the great wealth endangered by his adherence to the cause of independence. "Nay," said another: "there are several Charles Carrolls -- he cannot be identified." Mr. Carroll, hearing the conversation, immediately added to his signature the words *of Carrollton*, the name of the estate on which he resided, remarking as he did so, "They cannot mistake me now."

powerhouse.

The formal signing of the Declaration established a clear-cut course toward liberty and equality for American Colonials. Even though the way toward final, certain independence lay along a desperate, stormy route far into the discernible future, the patriots had firmly determined the direction to be taken, in the face of staggering odds. The risks and cost burdens shouldered by the patriots at Philadelphia cannot be truly measured today. But they were quite clearly grasped by many others in Western European nations who deeply appreciated what the American Colonials were willing to fight for in a politically sacred cause that surpassed even the struggles of ancient Greeks and Romans toward the dignity of man upheld in newly created nations and city states where democracy and republican government were realized only after centuries of protest and painful sacrifice of the many born into the lower levels of society and total slavery.

From the earliest American challenges to British sovereignty because of newly imposed economic and political strictures, taxes and military force, many of the European crusaders against royal despotism and absolutism took courage. They were amazed at the spiritual strength, unity and audacity that motivated Britain's North American colonies as they dared to unilaterally declare themselves no longer obliged to accept an overseas monarch as their head of state. Even Parliament voices expressed surprise and support for Britain's colonial brothers across the sea who dared to act as those in Europe could not afford to do under the ever present and powerful noses of the "God-annointed" monarchs. [46]

The North American revolutionary cause was seen as a very just one throughout most of western civilization. One French historian of the 18th Century wrote that the Declaration of Independence had an immense effect . . . The cause was so noble and the effort was so grand, that there was not a doubt, not a hesitation, in the sentiment of the entire world, and that governments and the rulers of States would seek glory by thinking like the American people. About mid-19th Century British historian Henry Buckle, sympathizing with the American Colonials,

---

46   *The Rise of the Republic, op.cit..*

This modern presentation copy of the Declaration of Independence is what National Archives offers now to the public. It is several clean-up-work-over generations beyond August 1, 1776. Note Signer Stone's signature in center just below that of John Hancock.

In CONGRESS, July 4, 1776.

The unanimous Declaration of the thirteen united States of America.

described them as
> *the great people who gloriously obtained their*
> *independence.*

And further, Buckle stated that
> *. . . The Declaration ought to be hung up in the*
> *nursery of every king, and blazoned on the porch of*
> *every royal palace.* [47]

Nobody can doubt that the influence of the Signers reached far beyond Philadelphia, and very quickly. The courage, patriotism and political skills of Stone and his brother Signers changed the nature of Western Civilization forever as for the first time ever the individual became responsible for and able to personally help shape his own destiny. And by like token, he largely bore for the first time responsibility for failures and weaknesses of his own creation.

The 1783 Treaty of Paris marked the final act that recognized a complete victory for the Americans in their long, excruciating drive toward achievement of the hopes, intentions and philosophies expressed in the Declaration of Independence. Now, fed with inspiration and hope generated by American success, peoples in most of Western Europe and the Western Hemisphere revolted against absolutist monarchs during the next century and a half – France, Italy, Germany, Russia and most of Latin America. And now, amazingly, as the door opens onto the Third Millennium, over a billion human beings still look toward America as a world role model for the most humane and popularly desirable features of liberty and self government.

Late in 2001 the National Archives and Records Service (NARS) slant on our Declaration of Independence world-wide impact was clearly stated
> *Nations begin in many ways; often in conflict*
> *between existing orders and those who challenge*
> *them in various forms of opposition. The birth of*
> *the United States included all of them, but was*
> *unique in the immensity of its influence on the*
> *course of history and development of democracy.*

---

47   Henry Buckle, *History of Civilization in England*, (London Edition, 1857,) i, p. 846. Hereinafter *History of Civilization*.

Ignition of stirring passions of the oppressed
occurred at a single place, at one time, and with
one remarkably well and boldly devised document
– the Declaration of Independence of the United
States of America. [48]

The NARS Declaration of Independence history includes a detailed account of the document's many journeys after the August 2, 1776 final signing in Philadelphia. Its very first trip out of Philadelphia was by light wagon to Baltimore in response to a threatened British capture of the capital city. Three months later it was taken back to Philadelphia. During the next 35 years this priceless parchment bounced around in and between five States for reasons of protection.

The Declaration's longest journey took place early in World War II when it, and other valuable national paper treasures were sent to Fort Knox, Kentucky for safety during the war. In an amazing connection with the Fort Knox move and the Stone family of southern Maryland a photographer at the Fort working for the U. S. Army Corps of Engineers took a close-up photograph of the Declaration at the Fort.

Photographer M. Truman Stone was a direct descendant of Governor William Stone of Poynton Manor and a descendant of an uncle of Thomas the Signer. Mr. Stone photographed the document May 2, 1942 using an F x 5 Speed Graphic. At its new home the Declaration was in equally distinguished company as it rested near the United States Constitution, the Magna Carta and the Gutenberg Bible, all sent there for wartime safekeeping. The Declaration underwent some repair and preservation work at Fort Knox under the supervision of Archibald MacLeish, who was the Librarian of Congress from 1939 until 1944. Truman Stone photographed the Declaration under the supervision of MacLeish.

---

48 National Archives and Records Service, *The Declaration of Independence – A History,* Website: http:www.nars.gov/exhall/charters/declaration/dechist. html, p.1

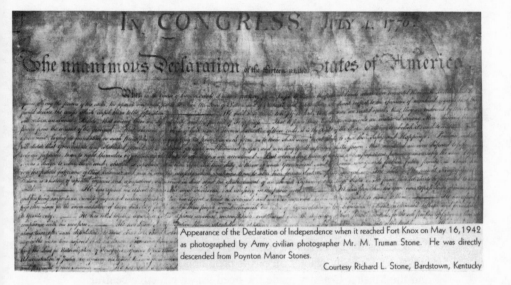

Appearance of the Declaration of Independence when it reached Fort Knox on May 16, 1942 as photographed by Army civilian photographer Mr. M. Truman Stone. He was directly descended from Poynton Manor Stones.

Courtesy Richard L. Stone, Bardstown, Kentucky

M. Truman Stone in 1942 at Fort Knox, Kentucky. He worked under Congressional Librarian Archibald MacLeish to monitor photographically the changing condition of the Declaration document during the early war years. Courtesy Richard L. Stone, Bardstown, Kentucky

Articles of Confederation Role

If ever a case were to be made for Thomas Stone having been a significant historical figure during the Revolutionary War period it should be based in great part on his support of the Articles of Confederation. A few sophisticated Revolutionary War period historians may have wondered who the "Thomas Stone" was whose signature appeared clearly on the Articles of Confederation initial draft of mid-1776. In June 1776 the Continental Congress appointed a committee from its membership to "prepare and digest the form of a confederation to be entered into between these States." This reflection of awareness of an urgent need for a cohesive central political entity to bind the colonies into a single machine of government in a way constituted a prediction of what was to happen on the second day of the next month. The concept of central government had been debated in two Continental Congresses for more than a year. However, the increasing pressures for early resolution of the problems between the colonies and the Mother Country made the need for an effective central government a very urgent one.

The new committee designated by Congress to work on the framework of confederation was dominated by John Dickinson, a capable and scholarly student of constitutional government. One delegate from each colony was appointed to work with this committee. Dickinson represented Delaware. Thomas Stone was asked to represent Maryland. Everything considered, this certainly was a measure of the trust and recognition given this quiet, humble, steady, capable man by his colleagues in Congress. The group worked quickly and had a draft ready for consideration by the Congress on July 12, 1776, in which is spelled out perhaps for the very first time the name of the new nation, "The United States of America." Thomas Stone's signature appeared on this first draft. In many ways this version was excellent, but it included provisions a bit too progressive for the moment, provisions that would become part of the 1787 Constitution. [49]

---

49 General Services Administration National Archives and Records Service, *Papers of the Continental Congress, 1771-1789*, Washington, DC. Micro-

However, the final Articles of Confederation were not accepted by Congress until July 9, 1778. Eight states ratified the articles almost immediately. Delaware held out until early 1779, leaving only Maryland and a few other small Colonies yet to ratify the agreement for confederation. [50] And this took two more years.

About 150 years ago historian John Sanderson with extraordinarily sensitive perception wrote that

> *there never was perhaps an undertaking of greater difficulty than the formation of the Confederacy at that period.*

And he went on to say that,

> *The peculiar responsibility of Mr. Stone, in being the only Maryland delegate in the committee, and the sentiments of Maryland being particularly hostile to the measure, unless with conditions that it was found impossible to obtain from the other States, may easily be appreciated.*

After the proposed articles were approved by Congress, that body sent a letter to the States urging adoption of the plan. The letter pointed out that this business,

> *equally intricate and important, has, in its progress, been attended with uncommon embarrassments and delay, which the most anxious solicitude and persevering diligence could not prevent.*

The letter also expressed Congress' opinion that the Articles of Confederation would

> *more than any other consideration . . . confound our foreign enemies, defeat the flagitious practices of the disaffected, strengthen and confirm our friends, . . . add weight and respect to our councils*

---

film Rolls 9, 22, 61 and 78 (84).

50 General Services Administration, Washington, DC, 1970 *The Formation of the Union,* National Archives Publication #7013. This excellent publication is a documentary history based upon an exhibit in the National Archives Building during the 1970 period. Hereinafter, *Formation.*

at home and to our treaties abroad.
In spite of the solid case widely made for ratification Maryland held back until early 1781. [51]

Stone's work with Pennsylvania's John Dickinson in drafting the Articles of Confederation turned out to be directly helpful to Marylanders struggling to draft the State's first Constitution in 1776. By this time Dickinson had become a widely acknowledged authority on constitutional government. Neither Stone nor Dickinson attended the Maryland Constitutional Convention, but their weight was felt during its deliberations. Stone had asked Dickinson to travel to Annapolis to advise the Convention, but matters in Congress required his full attention there. And Thomas Stone himself did not directly participate because of illness. However, Dickinson kept closely in touch with Annapolis during the convention and furnished welcome guidance. Stone felt that Dickinson could help Maryland form a

> . . . *constitution upon permanent first principles . . .*
> *I think it not improbable that a well formed*
> *government in a state so near* [to Philadelphia] *as*
> *Maryland might tend to restore the affairs of this*
> [country] . . .

Most assuredly, John Dickinson felt the absence of Thomas Stone at the Philadelphia Convention in 1787. [52]

Stone was re-elected to Congress in February 1777 but did not attend. The same month he declined to continue congressional service. He had quite regularly attended sessions of the First and Second Continental Congresses since first elected in December 1774. Stone remained long enough to see the Articles of Confederation approved by Congress. He did not again take a seat in Congress until March 1784, three years after Maryland's ratification.

Most of Thomas Stone's political life was at the state level from 1777 through 1786. He served in the Senate from the very

---

51 *Sanderson, Lives of the Signers, op.cit.* 9: pp. 163, 165.

52 Edward C. Papenfuse, State Archivist (Md.) and Commissioner of Land Patents letter to the Honorable William S. James, State Treasurer, Annapolis, June 5, 1986.

beginning of Maryland's new state government, remaining there from 1776 through 1786, with but one short interruption.

He was elected in Charles County in 1780 to serve in the House of Delegates to fill a vacancy, but he resigned from that House December 26 the same year. From then on he again sat in the Senate, Western Shore, for the term of 1781-1786. [53]

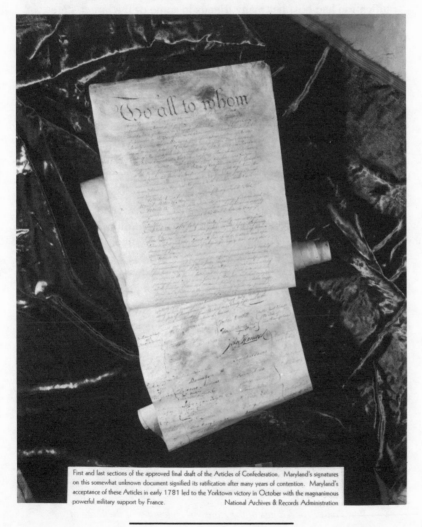

First and last sections of the approved final draft of the Articles of Confederation. Maryland's signatures on this somewhat unknown document signified its ratification after many years of contention. Maryland's acceptance of these Articles in early 1781 led to the Yorktown victory in October with the magnanimous powerful military support by France.   National Archives & Records Administration

53   *MHR Biographical Dictionary, op.cit.*   2: **pp. 787-788.**

Ratification of the Articles

Stone's return to the State seat of power in Annapolis turned out to be important almost beyond measure with respect to creation of the new federal government under the Articles of Confederation. Maryland's long, unwavering obstinacy over ratification had cost her many friends in some of the larger states. A few of the smaller states, however, supported Maryland's rejection stand. It hinged primarily on Maryland's fears that the western lands long claimed by several of the larger states (based on early Crown charters) would in years to come make them unacceptably prosperous and politically powerful in the proposed new central government. Marylanders felt very uneasy about being part of a government in which they and a few other small states would surely and continuously lose strength and prestige.

Charles County born John Hanson (first President of the United States in Congress Assembled) and Thomas Stone fought for about three years to convince the larger states with western land claims that they should surrender them to the new central authority, so that all former colonies might stand to benefit ultimately by the settlement and management of these lands. Finally, in the Maryland Assembly of 1780-1781, things came to a head -- in part because of former governor Thomas Johnson's staunch advocacy of Maryland ratifying the Articles. [54] In 1780 the course of the war took a sudden and disturbing turn with the southern states being invaded by major, victorious British military forces. General Rochambeau with 5000 French army regulars arrived that same year in Rhode Island. It wasn't until a year later, however, that American and French troops joined in a long overland march to Virginia to face British forces that had wreaked havoc for over a year in the southern colonies, handing American armies several stinging, demoralizing defeats. It began to appear to the Maryland Assembly that it might be time to ratify the Articles of Confederation, as ---

---

54   *Votes and Proceedings of the House of Delegates of the State of Maryland - October session, 1780 being the first session of this assembly,* pp. 42, 45. Hereinafter *V & P House.*

*it is said that the common enemy are encouraged to
hope that the Union may be dissolved, unless this
State confederates . . . and that our friends and
illustrious allies are impressed with an idea that the
common cause would be promoted by this State
formally acceding to the Confederation.* [55]

About this time the matter of the western land claims
controversy had begun to seem much less of a problem since
Virginia, New York and Connecticut were now offering to
relinquish their claims in favor of the new national central authority.
Reflecting this and other changes in national attitude the Maryland
House of Delegates on January 27, 1781, voted for ratification.[56]
However, the next day the Senate vote was negative, with nine
senators voting, including Thomas Stone. [57] With Thomas Johnson
working in the House of Delegates and Thomas Stone, his loyal
friend and political ally, working in the Senate ratification stood its
best chance ever. There existed one big stumbling block. Thomas
Stone's extremely influential and already legendary uncle, Daniel of
St. Thomas Jenifer, continued to preside over the Senate. It was no
secret anywhere that Jenifer had long been disenchanted with the
prospect of just about any form of central political authority for the
colonies. Late on the date of the negative vote the House of
Delegates sent their colleagues in the Senate a message that
Maryland's ratification would not damage the State's position with
respect to the western lands and that indeed continued obstinacy

---

55   St. George L. Sioussat, "The Chevalier de la Luzerne and the Ratification
of the Articles of Confederation by Maryland, 1780-1781." Offprint from *The
Pennsylvania Magazine of History and Biography,* Philadelphia, PA., October
1936, pp. 405-418. This quotation is from an early 1781 House of Delegates
resolution, a clear indication of Maryland's turnabout in her view of
ratification, and quite possibly the words of Thomas Johnson. Hereinafter,
Sioussat, Luzerne.

56 .   *V & P House, op.cit.*   January 27, 1781, pp. 104-109.

57 *Votes and Proceedings of the Senate of the State of Maryland,* January 28,
1781, pp. 38-40. Hereinafter *V & P Senate.*

71

might do serious harm. They argued that ratification by their State

> *will, in all probability spread confidence and*
> *satisfaction amongst the States, gratify the wish of*
> *our illustrious ally* [France], *and may make us to be*
> *considered by our enemy* [Britain], *and all Europe*
> *as one firm cemented body."* [58]

Late in 1780 Maryland statesmen Thomas Johnson,
Matthew Tilghman, Samuel Chase; Charles Carroll and Thomas
Stone understood the Articles of Confederation constituted a
moribund political instrument. And this condition was the first
order of business in the Assembly of Maryland. The gravity of this
lured Thomas Johnson from retirement and he, with energetic
support from Stone, pushed Maryland onto the highway toward
ratification. This had been bogged down since Congress had
approved the Articles July 9, 1778. Maryland, Delaware, and New
Jersey had been ratification hold-outs until 1779. Only Maryland
remained obdurate until 1781. The claims of some large States to
western lands still worried Marylanders. They felt strongly that
land west of the Appalachians should belong to the new central
government of the United States of America. An opening wedge
came in February 1780 when New York relinquished her claims to
western lands. Then, Virginia in early January 1781 agreed to
surrender her claims to western lands after holding firm for years.
After this, Johnson and Stone felt Maryland's view of ratification
should change and that Maryland ratification must occur quickly.
When the first vote was taken in the Senate only four senators,
including Stone, voted for ratification. The Senate vote against
ratification was not the end of things. Senate President Daniel of
St. Thomas Jenifer voted against ratification, breaking a tie vote. [59]
Thomas Johnson needled the Senate now -- telling them in effect
their vote was all standing between the chaos of the existing central
government and the blessings of a working central political
authority. The Senate moved quickly to match the House of
Delegate's approval -- with Thomas Stone bringing his full powers

---

58.   *V & P House, op.cit.*.

59   *V & P Senate, op.cit.* October Session, 1780, p. 380.

of intellect, reason, and political skills to bear on the recalcitrant State Senate. The Senate approved January 30, 1781. It has been correctly said that Maryland's attitude toward western lands management truly led the way toward a strong, respected Federal Government. [60]

This January 30, 1781 letter removed the last hurdle in the way of ratification. It was signed by the Senate clerk, but the writing is in the incisiveness, quality, political savoir-faire and construction – usually attributed to Thomas Stone. It is broadly conceded now that Stone wrote many of the reports issued by committees and councils in which he served. One of America's most valuable public documents, the Senate approval prepared the way to Philadelphia, but over very rocky ground.

> *By the SENATE,*
>
> *January 30, 1781.*
>
> *Gentlemen,*
>
> *At the earnest desire of your house we have again taken up the bill to empower the delegates in congress to subscribe and ratify the articles of confederation. You cannot be unacquainted with those reasons which have hitherto influenced this state to with-hold her assent to those articles. It has been generally supposed, and in our opinion upon good grounds, that the claim of this state to a proportionable part of the western country can be better supported under the present form of union, than that of the confederation; influenced by this opinion, we put our negative on the bill; but being sensible that a confederation is anxiously desired by every friend to the future peace and happiness of these United States, and as the pressing exigencies of our affairs demand the adoption of every measure that promises in the smallest degree to strengthen our cause and produce confidence and satisfaction among the several states, and as the*

---

60   John Fiske, *Critical Period of American History*, New York and Boston, 1886. p. 192. Hereinafter, *Critical Period.*.

*powers given to the delegates by the bill, in your
opinion, cannot alter or injure our claim to the
western country, but that claim may be as fully
ascertained and as firmly secured after as before
the confederation; and as we rely on the justice and
disposition of congress hereafter for the
establishment of our claim, and to defeat the hopes
of our enemy, and gratify the earnest desire of your
house, we have returned you the bill with our
affirmative. We most earnestly wish this measure
may be productive of all the good you expect from
it, but should it be attended with ill effects, we shall
be so far from imputing them to you, that we shall
always hold ourselves equally responsible for the
consequences of this important measure, which we
are satisfied is taken with the most virtuous
intentions.*

By order,

J. MACCUBBIN, clk.

The powerful, persuasive, House of Delegates message to
the upper house was very convincing. On January 30, the Senate
voted to ratify, but under rather peculiar circumstances. The day
before, Senate President Jenifer, being "indisposed and unable to
attend," was absent. George Plater presided in his stead.
Considering Jenifer's feelings about ratification and the great
prestige he enjoyed in the Assembly it was felt that his absence of
itself may have been contrived. Perhaps Jenifer deliberately
removed himself from the arena because he was unwilling to
oppose two people whom he respected greatly -- nephew Thomas
Stone and Thomas Johnson who spearheaded the fight for
ratification in the House of Delegates. So in a rather oblique way
Thomas Stone may have controlled the Senate's swing vote that led
to the ratification of the Articles of Confederation and the resulting
establishment of the first central political authority in the new
United States of America. [61] Surely Jenifer knew the depth of his
nephew's commitment to the Articles of Confederation, which he

---

61 *V & P Senate, op.cit.* PP. 39, 41.

had worked so hard to form and promote during the latter half of 1776. Also, possibly Stone's cris-crossing from one chamber to the other during the period of this 1780-1781 Assembly had to do with strategy. After all, when it came time for a critical vote the two most powerful Maryland friends of ratification were Johnson in the House and Stone in the Senate, each in a strategic position of knowledge and influence. On February 22, 1781, Governor Thomas Sim Lee signed the bill, the final act to assure ratification of the Articles, after nearly five years of "nation"-wide dissension about the matter of a potent central political authority that might create a viable nation-state out of chaos and doubt.

Historian John Fiske, in *Critical Period of American History*, stated in this work

> *. . . of the State hold-outs on ratification only Maryland fairly rose to the occasion . . .*
> *in a well-directed display of statesmanship – suggesting an idea, startling at first, but from which substantial positive results followed – all the way to the Philadelphia Convention. And by her resolution to withhold ratification on behalf of herself and other small states Maryland showed the way toward creation of the new Federal Constitution in 1787.*

So the deliberations of the Maryland assembly in the 1780-81 session placed a sound cornerstone in the structure of the new union. [62]

Daniel of St. Thomas Jenifer continued to have profound reservations about the impact of the new central government. In a letter he wrote to John Hall of Philadelphia July 24, 1781, he said that

> *our great Estate as you call it remains in the same situation as it did before the confederation, indeed I think in a much worse. The adoption of that measure after* [Maryland] *holding out so long will I fear be productive of many ills, . . .* [63]

---

62 *Critical Period, op.cit..*

63 Quoted in Sioussat, *The Chevalier de la Luzerne,* pp. 405, 406.

An interesting and revealing letter of November 19, 1788 from Thomas's son, Frederick, in Annapolis to Uncle Walter (Port Tobacco merchant) mentions Daniel of St. Thomas Jenifer's attitude toward the new Federal government spawned by the 1787 Philadelphia Convention. Although Jenifer signed the Constitution for Maryland he harbored negative thoughts about a new, powerful Head-of-State mechanism. Frederick told Walter about the Assembly's effort to select a new governor

> *. . . it was thought that Major Jenifer would be elected, but I believe he has changed the face of affairs again by betraying some Anti-Federal Principals.*

However, Frederick feels the Major may yet succeed to the governorship. Jenifer died in 1790 not having experienced the honor of leading his native State. [64]

---

64 Maryland Historical Society, Baltimore, MD, letter Frederick Stone to Walter Stone, November 19, 1788, MS 406. Hereinafter, *MHS 406.*

The Mount Vernon Convention

In Annapolis on January 28, 1785, Thomas Stone wrote a significant letter, in a clear, careful hand, to an old acquaintance at Mount Vernon, the honorable George Washington

It gives me much pleasure to know that our act [of Maryland] for opening the navigation of Potomack arrived in time to be adopted by the Assembly of Virginia. If the scheme is properly executed I have the most sanguine expectation that it will fully succeed to the wishes of those who are anxious to promote the wellfare [sic] of these States and to form a strong chain of connection between the western and Atlantic [state] governments. Mr. Jenifer, Johnson, Chase and myself are appointed commissioners to settle the jurisdiction and navigation of the bay and the rivers Potomack and Pocomoke with the commissioners of Virginia. We have also instructions to make application to Pennsylvania for leave to clear a road from Potomack to the western waters. Our Assembly proposes the meeting of the commissioners to be on the 21st of March at Alexandria if agreeable to the commissioners of Virginia. I have no doubt but the subjects of our mission will be settled to mutual satisfaction. It will add much to the satisfaction I shall feel in discharging this trust that I shall have an opportunity of paying my respects to you at Mount Vernon, which I have long wished to do, but in truth the necessary attention to professional and public business have kept me so closely employed that I have never had a time when I could gratify my inclination without neglecting some duty which I was particularly bound to perform. I hope nevertheless that you will do me the justice to believe that I warmly participate in the high regard and esteem in which you are held by all the friends of this country and that I am Sir with sentiments of very sincere attachment, your most obediant [sic] and most humble servant, T. Stone. [65]

This letter is very revealing in more than one respect. It is probably as good an example of the quality and overall skill Stone could bring to bear in written communication. It is clear, the tone is one of great sensitivity and respect, and it displays a comprehension of major national issues of the time. It is an instrument that reflects the degree of intellect, statesmanship and craft that Stone had been able for years to combine in his approach to dealing with people at any level of society and government.

A further revelation is that Stone was called upon by Maryland's Governor William Paca, Stone's old Continental Congress peer and Signer, and the Assembly to announce to the estimable Washington Maryland's proposal for the Alexandria-Mount Vernon convention. Maryland's view of the import of the planned meeting in Virginia is explicit in the election of extremely capable representatives appointed to speak for the state: Jenifer, Johnson, Chase and Stone together constituted an elite, prestigious and powerful company. Stone served as "point man" in putting this affair in motion through his respectful but slightly prodding letter to Mount Vernon.

Nearly eight years earlier Daniel of St. Thomas Jenifer had penned a carefully constructed, brief letter to (probably) the Virginia General Assembly Gentlemen. It was Maryland's effort to arrange a meeting between some Maryland and Virginia delegates

> . . . *for the purpose of setting the navigation of,*
> *and jurisdiction over that part of Chesapeake Bay*
> *which lies within the limits of Virginia and over the*
> *rivers Potomack and Pocomoke* . . .

Jenifer proposes a meeting at Alexandria, Virginia the 2nd of February, 1778. Stone's letter on the same subject followed eight years later, and Virginia still was not prepared to discuss increasingly grave problems of major concern to both states.

The Alexandria Conference, frequently called the Mount Vernon Conference, was held in March 1785, as suggested by the

---

65   Gratz Autograph Collection, Historical Society of Pennsylvania, Philadelphia. Thomas Stone to George Washington, January 28, 1785, Folio P.1.s, case 1, box 11. Hereinafter, *Gratz.*

Assembly of Maryland. Most of the deliberations of the Convention were held at Mount Vernon, where as guests of General Washington the Maryland Commission helped draft a thirteen-part compact that would significantly increase cooperation between the two States on matters of mutual commercial interest. This successful meeting is said to have led to a call for the "Annapolis Convention," which was held at Annapolis in the fall of 1786. Then, in turn, **this** meeting produced a proposal for a general all-states convention to be held at Philadelphia in May 1787. Oddly, and perhaps unfortunately, the Maryland Assembly chose not to send delegates to the Annapolis Convention, but not without some rather sound rationalization. It is beyond credibility that Stone in Annapolis did not monitor the deliberations of the Convention. His role likely was one more of substance than form. Surely he felt about the success of the Annapolis meeting no less than he struggled for a happy outcome of the Mount Vernon Convention. Had Thomas Stone participated in the Philadelphia Convention it would have been a significant final link in a nationally short chain of events that he helped launch as a major participant at Mount Vernon more than two years earlier. [66]

The significance of the Mount Vernon Convention has been underestimated by many scholars. It served as an essential first step toward our final form of national government under today's Constitution. Its significance can be placed in appropriate perspective only when it is considered in the light of the desperate times under the Articles of Confederation. Already in the spring of 1785 the Peace of Paris and the infirm condition of the government under the Articles were deeply disappointing to many Americans. Now many thoughtful patriotic men of intellect and political understanding felt the new nation was crumbling around them when yet hardly off the ground. The government could not collect internal revenues, and with an empty treasury found itself helpless and facing bankruptcy. Even worse, it faced broad public defiance of its authority. The Mount Vernon Convention brought together a few men who knew what was happening and feared rightfully for

---

66 David C. Roller & Robert W. Twyman, eds., *The Encyclopedia of Southern History*. Baton Rouge & London, 1979. P. 36.

the future of the new republic. When the convention ended March
29 host George Washington noted in his diary for that day that

> *Major Jenifer, Mr. Stone, and Mr.* [Alexander]
> *Henderson* [of Virginia] *went away before breakfast
> and Co.* [George] *Mason* [of Virginia] *in my
> carriage after it.* [67]

*The Mount Vernon Conference: First Step Toward
Philadelphia* leads into a perceptive article by Richard B. Morris
whose astute observation deserves attention now

> *An unusual convergence of issues drawn from
> history, geography and technology, and initially
> involving just two states, began the chain of events
> that drew twelve of the thirteen states to
> Philadelphia in May of 1787.*

The author quite correctly points out that Maryland was
much better prepared to deal with Convention issues than was poor
Virginia, which seemed quite unable to put its act together and get
ready to deal with the major issues that were the very purpose of
the meeting. In fact, when the Maryland delegation arrived March
21 at Alexandria they found no Virginia gentlemen there to
welcome them.   The scope of matters taken up at Mount Vernon
raised questions of broad national import directly related to the
inadequacies of the Articles of Confederation as the central
machinery of government. Corrosive issues of trade, currency,
navigation, debt collection and duties created serious problems that
could not be managed under the Articles. These issues made it
clear that much had to be done, and soon, to salvage the new
National Government structure to check disaster that doubtless
would destroy all that purchased by the American Revolution. [68]

---

67   Donald Jackson & Dorothy Twohig, Eds., *The Diaries of George
Washington* Vol. IV, 1784-June 1786. Charlottesville, VA, 1978. P. 109.
[The Maryland commissioners arrived at Mount Vernon on Friday p.m.,
March 25.]

68   Richard B. Morris, *The Mount Vernon Conference: First Step Toward
Philadelphia*, Mount Vernon, VA. Written in support of the 1985 observance
at Mount Vernon of the 1785 Convention. Mr. Morris is a professor of history
emeritus at Columbia University.

An early aspect of Mount Vernon as it probably
looked in 1785 during the Mount Vernon
Convention deliberations. By historian Benson J.
Lossing, c. 1830.

*The Mount Vernon Ladies' Association of the Union
Annual Report for 1985* reflects a healthy comprehension of where
the Mount Vernon deliberations led. Success of this meeting
pointed directly toward the 1787 Philadelphia Convention of
representatives from each state. The report leads into its body with
the caption ". . . Prelude to the Constitution: The Mount Vernon
Conference of 1785." Sadly, no mention was made in this report
about how Maryland, sparked by the Stone letter to Washington,
forced the issue and insisted on a two-State meeting to resolve Bay
and river jurisdictional problems. Convention accounts indicate
how poorly prepared the Virginians were for the meeting. Only the
Maryland team arrived complete and on schedule . . . March 21,
1785. The delegates left Alexandria March 25 and met at Mount
Vernon to enter into their deliberations at the invitation of
Washington. Here Washington the host did not take part in the

---

Convention labors which brought forth a magnificent document --
The Potomac River Compact, which at the beginning of the 21st
century still insures justice, order and control to all those who travel
the Chesapeake Bay and the several major rivers that flow into it.
Speaking for Maryland were Daniel of St. Thomas Jenifer, Samuel
Chase and Thomas Stone. Stone's close friend Thomas Johnson
was appointed the fourth Marylander to participate at Mount
Vernon, but he failed to get there. [69]

Under a sub-head titled *Movement to Strengthen the
National Government,* writers at the National Archives placed the
Mount Vernon outcome in fair perspective

*Where there was a disagreement between two States
about trade they had to negotiate the matter much
as two independent nations may have done.*

In early 1785, Virginia and Maryland successfully settled their
dispute over commerce and navigation on Chesapeake Bay through
an inter-state agreement at the Mount Vernon Convention. Well
pleased with the results the Virginia Legislature in 1786 proposed a
convention to consider commercial problems among **all** the former
Colonies. This led to the Annapolis meeting in 1786. Only five
States were represented here, but the doorway leading to
Philadelphia as a result of the Annapolis meeting set the stage for
the much larger Convention to open in May the next year. [70]

Records of the Votes and Proceedings, House of Delegates,
for November 1786 indicate that Thomas Stone was intimately
involved in the Assembly in Maryland's preparation to participate in
"a Convention to be held in the City of Philadelphia in the month of
May next, for the purpose of revising the Federal Constitution."
Thomas Stone appears to have been a major link in maintaining
communication in this matter between the houses of the
Assembly. [71]

About two months after the Mount Vernon Convention,

---

69   *Mount Vernon Ladies' Association of the Union: 1985 Annual Report.*
(Mount Vernon, VA., 1985.)

70   *Formation, op.cit.*

71   *V & P House, op.cit.,* December 1786.

George Washington's long-proposed Potomac Company came into being with Washington as its first president. The purpose of the company was construction of a canal along the Potomac, much on the Virginia side, from Alexandria well into western Maryland. It was eventually to be the major navigation-road link that would reach the Ohio River and open up western lands to relatively safe, easy connections to east coast industry and agriculture. The company, jointly owned by Virginia and Maryland, was thought to become a major effort toward much greater commercial stability and prosperity in the new struggling United States. Thomas Stone was one of three Maryland Senate members who represented the State in the deliberations that led to approval of the Potomac Company. [72]

On December 3, 1785, George Washington wrote a letter to Charles Carroll and Thomas Stone on behalf of the directors of the Potomac Company reporting on an inspection of the terrain at both the Great Falls and Little Falls of the Potomac. It was around these falls that the company was planning to build a canal and locks to make it possible to navigate the Potomac as far west as navigable waters might be found. Apparently, the Assemblies of both Virginia and Maryland had a say in the construction of the canal because at this time Washington is asking Carroll and Stone to deal with the Maryland Assembly with respect to the desired minimum depth of the projected new waterway. Planners had felt originally that a four-foot depth would be adequate. After a survey of terrain conditions (much stone) near the falls of the Potomac, however, it was thought that a four-foot depth would be too costly. The assemblies of both States were asked by the company to approve a less expensive two-foot depth. [73]

Stone wrote from Annapolis December 10, replying to Washington's letter of the 3rd. He said that before Washington's letter was written the action of the Assembly requested by

---

72   Andrews, *op.cit.*, p. 637.

73   Library of Congress, Manuscript Division, Washington, D.C., letter from G. Washington to the Honorable Charles Carroll and the Honorable Thomas Stone, December 3, 1785.

Washington had already been taken and a copy of the Maryland Act had been sent to the Virginia Assembly. Stone goes on to tell Washington that the Compact made at Mount Vernon was ratified by the Maryland Assembly without dissenting vote in either House—

> . . . I hope it will meet with a friendly reception in
> your Assembly – I beg you will be assured that it
> will always give me particular pleasure to receive
> your communications and to gratify your wishes,
> being with very sincere respect and esteem, dear sir,
> your most obedient servant, T. Stone.

Once again, Thomas Stone handled on behalf of the Governor and Assembly of Maryland important official communications with George Washington. [74]

Early in 1787 Stone struggled with a new issue in the Assembly of Maryland that upset him very much. The subject was the issuance of paper money to be used in lieu of "traditional hard specie." He felt the need for discussing his personal feelings about this with someone perhaps more knowledgeable than he on the subject. So on January 30, 1787, Stone wrote to the man he respected perhaps more than any other, General Washington. He told Washington in his very short note that

> The Senate and House of Delegates of Maryland
> having differed upon the subject of issuing paper
> money on loan and the latter having appealed to the
> people I take the liberty of enclosing [for] you the
> papers of each House and if not disagreeable I
> shall be much obliged by a communication of your
> sentiments upon a subject which is likely to create
> great and perhaps dangerous divisions in this State,
> and am with perfect esteem, Sir, your most obedient
> servant, T. Stone.

Washington quickly replied. On February 16 he wrote at Mount Vernon that in general he agreed with Stone. He had the same fears and reservations about the efficacy of paper money.

---

74 John S. H. Fogg Autograph Collection, Maine Historical Society, Portland, Maine, letter from Thomas Stone to George Washington, December 10, 1785. Hereinafter, *Fogg*.

Washington stated

> . . . *I do not scruple to declare that, if I had a voice*
> *in your Legislature it would have been given*
> *decidedly against a paper emission upon the*
> *general principles of its utility as a representative*
> *and the necessity of it as a medium -- And as far as*
> *I have been able to understand its advocates for the*
> *two papers you sent me were the same and*
> *contained no reasons of the House of Delegates for*
> *the local want of it* [paper money] *in your State*
> *though I have seen and given them a cursory*
> *reading elsewhere, I should have been very little*
> *less opposed to it.*

Washington then expresses his fears that

> . . . *paper money issuance leads to inflation. The*
> *appreciation keeps pace with the quantum of the*
> *emission; and articles for which it is exchanged rise*
> *in a greater ration than the sinking value of the*
> *money -- wherein then is the farmer, the planter, the*
> *artizan* [sic] *benefitted?*

In other words, "the great man of Mount Vernon" gave Thomas
Stone of Maryland much comfort in this matter, which most
assuredly gave this Charles County legislator the wherewithal to
continue the fight against paper money for Maryland. [75]

Conjectural scene – Washington and a visitor chatting
at Mount Vernon in late 18th century. Engraving
possibly of artwork by Benson J. Lossing. Such
scenes likely occurred many times during the
Convention of March 1785.

---

75   Library of Congress, Manuscript Division, letter Thomas Stone to George
Washington, January 30, 1787, and George Washington to Thomas Stone,
February 16, 1787.

The Personal Business Side

As 1785 drew to a close, Stone, in a letter dated December 21, again exhorted his young brother to raise as much money in Charles County as possible

> *If Clarke has not paid interest due on his bond issue a writ -- sell hogs -- sell negroes as soon as possible . . . Make sure those hired out are well clothed.*

He shows great irritation over a Charles County slave owner who has accused him of fraud in the sale of an unwell slave, threatening to sue Stone. He tells Walter

> *. . . if he does I shall certainly treat him as he would not wish. My brother Michael told me he had informed the bidders as I desired him, that Sam had been subject to fits and that the sale was made on this information publicly given . . . Let any honest man determine whether the sale was not open and fair with full information. Inform purchaser I will not be trifled with*

Stone then tells Walter that

> *I want money, accordingly I must request you to raise as much as you can for me.*

On January 15 the next year Thomas told Walter

> *You will do what appears to you most proper with respect to the mill -- whatever agreement you make let it be in writing.*

One of the latest and most interesting Thomas Stone business documents surviving is an item entitled "Articles of Agreement," drawn up January 10, 1787, between Walter Stone for Thomas Stone and Thomas Ostro the Port Tobacco miller. Ostro, in spite of earlier threats to leave the mill, apparently decided to continue through 1787 and for this year Thomas Stone bound him tightly so that his management of the mill might be entirely to its owner's liking and favor. Stone's mill apparently was quite a large and successful establishment and included livestock and at least one slave. Ostro was committed by the new agreement to raising hogs and to finding horses to work fields. This was a twenty-acre parcel located on Port Tobacco Creek very close to Port Tobacco village. Ostro was allowed one-tenth of the clear profits of the mill and one-fifth of the pork raised, but not over 5,000 pounds for one year, plus one-half the profits from crops grown on the mill property. Also, the miller had

> to do justice to all customers and keep the mill in
> good and proper repair,

and through the agreement obliges himself to

> treat and use the negroes of said Stone, which may
> be at the mill, with care and humanity . . .

And there was to be absolutely no drinking or gaming at the mill and the

> . . . said Stone shall have free liberty to turn off the
> said Ostro at any time if he in any manner
> misbehaves himself -- of which the said Stone shall
> be the sole judge . . .   [76]

Apparently at this time Stone's mill manager at Port Tobacco, Thomas Ostro, felt he was not getting a large enough share of the toll and threatened to leave the mill. Stone expresses considerable concern over the mill and fears that Ostro will take away with him things not properly his. [77]

---

[76] *Wanamaker Scrapbook*, Historical Society of Pennsylvania, Philadelphia, p. 49.

[77] Library of Congress, Washington, DC, *The Stone Family of Maryland* collection. One of the very few existing windows that open onto the rather intimate life of the reserved, introspective Thomas are allowed us by a collection of family papers (137 individual items) in the possession of the Library of Congress. This package of correspondence contains many pieces addressed to or from Walter, a merchant at Port Tobacco, 1783-1791. Walter's will left his desk and papers to brother Michael Jenifer. Michael's son, another Michael Jenifer became a physician. After Dr. Michael's marriage he built Sunnyside in the Aquasco area of nearby Prince George's county. It is possible that the papers remained at Habre de Venture until about 1890 when Margaret Graham Stone gave them to Dr. Michael's son, Thomas, who farmed Sunnyside for his family and Habre de Venture for cousin Margaret. About 1910 the collection was put into the hands of Miss Grace Stone who was a granddaughter of Congressman Michael Jenifer Stone, a younger brother of Thomas. The papers were sent to her by a sister, Sue Colton of Aquasco,

For about eight years Thomas and John Hoskins Stone had placed incredible pressures on brother Walter – both pleading much of the time for Walter's help in raising money for them. During these years he probably lived at Habre de Venture, at least after 1783. [78]

While living in Annapolis, heavily occupied with complex affairs of state and national governments, Thomas Stone tried to keep up with his Annapolis law practice and court business in Charles County at the same time, not always successfully. In the November 8, 1786 issue of the *Maryland Gazette* Walter Hanson, John Dent, Samuel Hanson, Jr. and Richard Barnes of Charles County issued jointly a "Whereas" type announcement that stated

> . . . *the business of Charles County court has been greatly retarded and delayed by the non-attendance of T. Stone, Esq. Practicing attorney of said court, whereby the docket has been loaded and swelled to*

Maryland, when Miss Grace lived at 732-9th St., N.E., Washington, D. C. They were presented to the Library of Congress shortly thereafter. Hereinafter cited as *LC Stone Family*.

78   *Ibid.* Letter from Walter J. Stone to Michael Jenifer Stone, undated but possibly 1791. One of the Stone family's saddest documents has to be this letter from Walter to his brother, Michael. For years Walter had suffered from a health problem he found totally disagreeable and physically distressing, as well as depressing. He had cut all ties to his steady, well compensated, Federal Government positions in Philadelphia and came home in 1783 to Port Tobacco. He kept store here for older brother, John Hoskins, for about eight years and handled much private business for brother Thomas after he moved to Annapolis about mid-1783. Prominent physicians Benjamin Rush in Philadelphia and Gustavus Richard Brown of Port Tobacco tried to heal Walter – but without success. Finally, it seems everything became overwhelming. A physician recommended that Walter "take the curative waters" at a then very popular and exclusive Virginia spa. He did – and died there in the fall of 1791. An event strongly hinted at in a letter to his brother – *"It is my desire that my horses be immediately sold to [help] pay Mr. Freeman, Mr. Maddox, and Mr. Ostro. I must beg my brothers to make up the deficit money. If I could have lived I should have paid, these are people under peculiar circumstances. I have suffered much, yet I wait my final end with confidence. Oh, my friends Religion ought to be our only pursuit. Your affectionate W. Stone."*

Margaret Brown Stone c. mid-1785 as done by Robert Edge Pine, probably while the Stones were living in the Peggy Stewart House in Annapolis.

National Portrait Gallery, Smithsonian Institution. Gift of Mrs. Frank J. Clements (nee March), a fifth generation descendant of Thomas and Margaret Stone.

The original mid-1785 portrait of Thomas Stone painted by Robert Edge Pine. Restored in 1973, this is the Pine portrait purchased by the City of Baltimore from Habre de Venture owner Michael Robertson Stone in 1928 along with the paneling. It had hung in the paneled parlor from c.1788-1928, always under the respectful care of the Stone family descendants of Michael Jenifer Stone.

Baltimore Museum of Art

a most enormous size, we therefore think proper to
give this public notice, that from this time no action
or suit will be delayed on account of the non-
attendance of the gentleman of the Bar . . .

Such uncomplimentary action by "old friends" in Charles
County greatly disturbed the Honorable Thomas Stone; in fact he
resented it mightily. In an unusually direct, forceful, well-written
letter printed in the *Maryland Gazette* of December 28, 1786,
Stone told the public that he considered the Charles County
complaint about his court in attendance to

. . . be considered a charge against me of
neglecting professional duties, which I did not
expect, even in this censorious age, it is proper I
should state facts to prevent any impression
injurious to me, being made by the assertions.

Stone also pointed out that

I have been a practicing lawyer in Charles County
court about 18 years and have attended every court
unless prevented by sickness or a necessary
attendance on public duty. To the best of my
recollection and belief, I attended all the courts of
that county for the year 1785; in the present year I
attended at April court, though the badness of the
weather prevented me from being at court until the
third day after it began. The weather was rainy, and
very, very little business could be done in the course
of the week. At June court I attended, the court was
adjourned the first day to the last week in August; it
being thought by the magistrates, and I believe
justly, that people would be much injured by taking
them from their crops, which were likely to suffer by
the consequences of great and continued rain. I
attended the adjourned court in August which sat a
week.
Being informed of a meeting of commissioners from
several states at Annapolis, on the first week in
*September, **and being appointed a commissioner***
for this state to confer with commissioners of

Virginia *upon particular subjects, I thought it my duty to be present. By the journey from Charles county to Annapolis I was so much fatigued and weakened, and in consequence so ill that I was altogether unable to attend the court the second week in September; and if I had been well, the state of uncertainty in which I was with respect to a conference with the commissioners of Virginia, or of the other states, would have detained me at Annapolis.* [Reference to the Annapolis Convention.] *Of these circumstances I informed the justices of Charles County court, and requested them to adjourn the court to a time in November, when I expected certainly to attend; the adjournment was made to the time proposed but the* [state] *general court continuing beyond that time, and I being engaged in trying causes in the general court, could not attend the county court without quitting the trials in which I was engaged in the superior court. I am not concerned in about half the causes* [incredible work load for one lawyer] *on the trial docket for Charles County, and my absence was certainly not the cause that the business in which I was not concerned was postponed. From these facts it will appear that the present state of the docket of Charles County court cannot justly be ascribed to my non-attendance. The accidental unfavourable weather in the court weeks of this year has been one cause to increase the trial docket, and the general practice of giving preference to the prosecution of the criminal business, which takes up great part of the week, will always render it impossible to finish the trials of each court without adjournment. The manner of conducting the business in future must depend upon the* **majority** *of the justices. I shall regularly attend the court, unless prevented by unavoidable accident, sickness, or superior duty, and if either of these causes should produce injury*

*to those who intrust me with their law business I
shall be extremely sorry, but can never esteem it a
proper consequence of accident, ill health, or public
service.*

*It is very disagreeable to be obliged to state in a
newspaper circumstances so uninteresting to the
public, but I hope it will be excused when silence
might be taken for acquiescence in an imputation
which I am conscious I do not deserve, and which I
had not the smallest reason to suppose would be
cast upon me by the subscribers to the
advertisement referred to, T. Stone, Annapolis,
December 17, 1786* [79]

In Annapolis the new Stone residence was a very short walk
from then already long-established King William's School, soon to
become St. John's College. It had been sheltered in the semi-divine
grace of the Archbishop of Canterbury since 1696. This year
marked the founding of King William's School in the center of
Annapolis. After a 1784 act established St. John's it joined old
King William's School. The merged college then became one with
the name St. John's. In 1784 St. John's began an urgently needed
money raising drive. Charles Carroll of Carrollton (thought to be
the richest man in America) gave $200.00. Thomas Stone, Samuel
Chase, and Daniel of St. Thomas Jenifer gave $100.00 each. On
February 28, 1786 an election for the St. John's Board of Visitors
was held in the Senate Room of the State House.

Thomas Stone was elected one of eight prominent men to
serve as Visitors and Governors of the college. Thomas's brother
John Hoskins Stone also was declared a Visitor at this time. [80]

Thomas Stone was one of five Visitors empowered to deal
with contracts needed in the starting of construction of St. John's
first new classroom building – converting a neglected building on
campus once planned to be a new State Capital building

---

79   *Maryland Gazette*, Annapolis, Maryland, December 28, 1786.

80   *Maryland Historical Magazine,* Baltimore, MD, June 1949, "The
Founding of St. John's College," pp. 82-83.

> *. . . a new institution . . . a grammar school to flourish within the already standing mouldering walls.*

Stone did not live to see the official 1787 college opening. [81]

McDowell Hall, oldest structure on St. John's College campus. Built in 1742 to serve as Maryland's Capitol, it stood seriously neglected until 1785 when it became destined for renovation to serve as the major college building. Its repair was overseen by Thomas Stone and several other prominent men who served as visitors for the new St. John's College.

Photo courtesy St. John's College, Annapolis

---

81   *Maryland Gazette*, Annapolis, MD, August 10, 1786 p.3. Also, St. John's College letter to author, June 29, 1987, Subj: Thomas Stone's support of the college.

The Last Years of Public Duties

Still a member of the State Senate, Thomas Stone was re-elected to Congress in November 1783. He was at the State House in Annapolis when General George Washington resigned his commission in December as commander-in-chief of the Army of the United States. He did not attend sessions of Congress in Philadelphia until March 1784. On March 26 of that year Charles Thomson, Jr., Secretary to the Congress, in bold hand noted for the record, that

> *Mr. Thomas Stone, a delegate for the State of*
> *Maryland attended and took his seat"* [82]

So began Thomas Stone's final stint of Federal service. He was kept very busy at least for a few months, serving on several committees for which he usually wrote final reports. One of Stone's greatest contributions now in Congress was his unique ability to write exceedingly well in a clear straightforward manner that usually did not reflect the common semantical convolutions of barrister-type prose. But his law background helped him develop a style especially appropriate for documents and formal communications of State. Stone's committee involvement brought him into many different roles, some petty, others exceedingly complex and significant.

In the *Papers of the Continental Congress* was an original report written by Stone about a petition of one Nathaniel Greenwood for back wages accruing while he was a prisoner of war. Stone served on a committee that considered measures about Mediterranean Passes, which were supposed to give American vessels unhindered passage through Mediterranean waters controlled (illegally, of course) by the Barbary Coast nations of northern Africa. These passes were to serve only until treaties could be arranged with the nations involved. The well-written report on this subject was authored by Stone. On another committee Stone wrote the final response to a request from the State of New York for Congress to indicate how many troops New

---

82   Emmet Collection, Rare Books & Manuscripts Div., New York, NY.

York had to furnish to garrison forts needed for the defense of that State.

At 4 o'clock on the afternoon of May 28, 1784, Congress had to elect a new chairman to serve when the president could not be there. Thomas Stone was elected by his peers in Congress. Then, on June 2, 1784, the Continental Congress (meeting in Congress Assembled) again elected Stone to be its temporary chairman. In this position he twice served as the Nation's Chief of State. Today, of course, the Vice President would have this honor. He also was serving on a committee that included Jacob Read, James Monroe, Hugh Williamson, and Roger Sherman, some of the most distinguished members of the Continental Congress at this time. [83]

Early in 1787 the Maryland Assembly appointed Thomas Stone to be a delegate to the Federal convention to be held in Philadelphia, starting in May of that year. He chose not to serve, probably because of his wife's now very serious illness, which appears to have been a crippling form of rheumatism. [84]

Somehow, during all the years of strenuous government service, national and state, Stone by 1783 had managed to accumulate considerable real estate holdings in Charles County. In addition to the Habre de Venture home estate, according to the 1783 tax assessment he owned five other properties nearby that totaled about 600 acres. Many people in this part of Maryland were land-poor at this time, but Stone's diversified total worth reflects a solid balance of real estate, slaves, silver plate, livestock, and other properties. Habre de Venture still consisted of its original 442 acres. Most of Stone's land was forested. As far as agricultural value was concerned much of his land was described in the 1783 tax assessment report as primarily "poor and/or barren, or stiff." The report shows that Habre de Venture had one good dwelling house, brick, a kitchen, and nine other necessary houses.

83　The above account of some of Stone's responsibilities and contributions through 1784 are from *Papers of the Continental Congress*, Nr. 32, pp. 127-133; Nr. 20 I, p. 401; Nr. 36 II, pp. 447, 451; and folio 557.

84　MHR, *op.cit. Biographical Dictionary*, 2: pp. 187, 188.

His Charles County lands were valued at 920 English pounds, and his slaves at 854 pounds. The total value of other properties amounted to 350 pounds. Including the value of "other" property Stone's total Charles County worth amounted to 2,331 pounds. [85] The life of a country lawyer seems to have treated him well to this point. During 1783 Stone would leave all this behind and move to a quite grand Annapolis mansion on Hanover Street, today in the shadow of the United States Naval Academy.

In 1773 Thomas Stone's father, David, died and the home plantation on the southeast corner of Poynton Manor went to Samuel, his oldest son by his first marriage. His father's death had a direct and very personal impact on Thomas's family life as long as he lived. As a result of it, Habre de Venture appears to have become a haven for younger brothers and sisters, some of whom doubtless had been sheltered at the Poynton Manor home of David before his death. These included (at least) the youngest child of David and Elizabeth, Walter Jenifer, born about 1760, and two sisters, Grace (never married), and Mrs. Catherine Scott, who moved into Habre de Venture with her son Alexander, born about 1770. Mrs. Scott was widowed some time during the Revolutionary War period, her husband dying at sea. At least three of this company still lived at Habre de Venture when Thomas died. Then, too, younger brother Michael Jenifer, the lawyer, probably lived at Habre de Venture on and off from 1783 until he married about 1794 and built his own home, Equality, about 1795 a few miles southeast of Port Tobacco. Michael conducted his law practice, at least in part, from Habre de Venture.

Doubtless through the good graces of brother Thomas young Walter found employment in Philadelphia about 1781 with Robert Morris's Office of Finance, part of the Confederation government. Walter held this job until late 1783, ending his government career with a short stint on the staff of Robert Livingston in the Office of Foreign Affairs. Unfortunately, Walter's life was a matter of considerable concern to Thomas. Both in Philadelphia and back in Port Tobacco where he went into

---

85   Archives of Maryland, Maryland Hall of Records, Annapolis, MD., 1783 Tax Assessment Record, Charles County. Hereinafter, *C. C. Tax Assessment.*

partnership with his older brother, John Hoskins, Walter suffered chronically poor health. In 1791, while "taking the waters" in Botetourt County, Virginia he died quite unexpectedly. He seems never to have matured fully nor settled down to any lifestyle that satisfied him in spite of long-range medical advice sent him by Dr. Benjamin Rush in Philadelphia . . . an acquaintance of brother Michael.

For a few years Walter's brothers, including Thomas, depended on him to handle family affairs in Charles County. [86] A peculiar combination of fortune and misfortune seems to have produced a remarkable legacy of rare Stone family documents in the Library of Congress. Almost beyond doubt they represent a personal collection of papers left at Habre de Venture by Walter. Certainly, had he known what fate had in store he might have done some discreet editing of the very personal material left at Habre de Venture when he set out for just a few days or weeks to test the curative waters. These papers include some scathing, sometimes raw descriptions in verse of young men and women who had been acquaintances, whether friend or enemy, principally in Philadelphia and Annapolis.

Perhaps more important for historians today are the few letters in this collection from Charles Carroll of Carrollton, Daniel of St. Thomas Jenifer, James Monroe, Robert Morris, and Dr. Benjamin Rush, in addition of course to those written and signed by Thomas himself. One rather early and interesting family item is a letter from Daniel of St. Thomas Jenifer to nephew Walter dated July 15, 1782 in which Jenifer mentions that he is going to continue acting as Intendant of Revenue (State Treasurer)

> *disagreeable as it may be in times when three*
> *fourths of the people have lost sight of the great*
> *object* [independence] *which inspired them to act in*
> *the beginning with such incomparable ardor.*

Jenifer also says he's glad that Walter's conduct has pleased Robert Morris.

By mid-1782 Thomas was writing to Walter about his (Walter's) wish to leave government and go into business, possibly

---

86   *LC-Stone Family, op.cit.*

at Port Tobacco. Thomas suggests to Walter that he enter into partnership with some importer in Philadelphia who could supply goods to a Port Tobacco business house. He suggests Walter pay for such produce with tobacco and other country items found cheaper in southern Maryland -- it could be a very profitable business. Thomas tells Walter that he has little prospect of being able to help his younger brother this year because of recent investments in land. He suggests that Walter remain with Mr. Morris at least through late fall. Thomas ends the letter,

All here join in love and best wishes to you.
The letter was written at Habre de Venture. [87]

On April 8, 1783, Thomas wrote to Walter from Port Tobacco giving him instructions for the building of a chariot being made in Philadelphia for Mrs. Stone by a highly respected craftsman, John Bringhurst. Apparently already anticipating a move into sophisticated, stylish Annapolis, Thomas had ordered a new chariot, a light, four-wheeled somewhat formal carriage. He says

> *I hope Binghurst* [sic] *will not go over their first price for the chariot -- I don't remember that I gave him any particular directions how to make it -- I don't want it very high nor very large -- neat, light and strong. Painted nearly the color of my phaeton if he can . . . paint it a kind of light green with a small mixture of blue . . . I don't want the chariot to have fashionable harness for four horses, etc. to go with postilions for the box . . . not for a man . . . who does not trust a driver on the box . . . must be content to adopt the other mode which is more safe . . . You know Mrs. Stone is not very tall even with a high headdress and therefore doesn't require such a very lofty top to her carriage . . . but I would incline it should not be quite so high as they are now made yet rather higher than the former fashion . . .* [88]

---

87   *Ibid.*

88   *Ibid.*

With some afterthought on April 26 Thomas again wrote to Walter about his new carriage, referring to the earlier letter. In particular he seemed concerned about the color. He says that

> *as to that point I leave it to you and the carriage maker, whatever colour is most fashionable and looks the best I would have. I want it a compleat [sic] good cariage [sic] for I would not have an indifferent one, but I am not for a gaudy and shewy [showy] one that will be stared at as a proof of the owner's vanity and folly.* [89]

Mr. Stone's comments about his new conveyance reflect the character of someone of quality, humility and social substance.

Late in 1783 the Thomas Stone family prepared to move to Annapolis, possibly because living conditions had grown uncomfortable at Habre de Venture and a growing law practice in the State capital now beckoned. Plans seemed well along by May. On the 29th of the month brother Michael Jenifer in Annapolis wrote to Walter in Philadelphia.

> *T.S. and myself are both still in Annapolis and are pretty well -- I believe he will come [move] to this place with his family in the course of the summer . . . . . We are all mightily cocked up with hopes that Congress will establish their residence in this city . . . . . The effects of the most glorious Peace [of Paris] are not as generaly [sic] seen or talkd [sic].* [90]

The day after Michael wrote to Walter a document was drawn up in Annapolis, dated May 20, 1783, through which Thomas Stone gained possession of his uncle's house at 207 Hanover Street in Annapolis, for which he promised to pay Daniel of St. Thomas Jenifer 4,500 pounds. The document indicates that this obligation "is to be void otherwise to remain in full force" should Stone and his family decide against possession of the Jenifer house and lots on Hanover Street. The document mentions lots B, I and G on the 1718 Stoddert plat of the said city, which adjoined

---

89   *Gratz, op.cit.*

90   *LC-Stone Family, op.cit.*

100

C. 1925 E. H. Pickering photograph of the Peggy Stewart House on Hanover Street in Annapolis. Built in 1751, this architectural gem was home to the Stones of Port Tobacco mid-1783 to mid-1787. From the front porch, owner Anthony Stewart could almost feel the heat from his burning brig, the *Peggy Stewart*, on October 19, 1774. So occurred Maryland's own "Boston Tea Party."

Enoch Pratt Free Library

lot H on which the dwelling house stood, and another lot on the north side of the street bought by Jenifer from Anthony Stewart. Other lots included in the transaction were on both the north and south sides of Hanover Street near the house. Lot H was the location of the Peggy Stewart House, where Jenifer and then Thomas and his family lived. Today this splendid brick town house is a National Historic Landmark. It must have been a "step-up" for the Stones. Even in 1783 such an abode offered many creature comforts seldom seen in rural Charles County. [91]

Here and there, years and miles apart, Thomas Stone steps into the light of fact through documents long in private hands. One letter to brother Walter dated 13 April 1783 in Philadelphia stated

> ... *We have received the long wished official information of a general peace* [of Paris] *being concluded at which we all most heartily rejoice. We must now set earnestly about paying our public debt ... and lay the foundation of happiness and security to posterity ...*

Stone also writes that he and his wife have been sick but are recovering . . . probably at Habre de Venture early in 1783

> ... *The attacks upon my old friend President* [John] *Dickinson are mere declamation as far as I have seen them ...*

Dickinson, an inspiration and constitutional government expert, had been a leader in preparation (1776-77) of the Articles of Confederation. From such grand height he fell quite flat in the eyes of many patriots when he chose not to sign the Declaration of Independence. [92]

In 1800 the executors for Thomas Stone's estate, his brother Michael J. and brother-in-law Gustavus R. Brown, came into Anne Arundel County court with a bill of complaint to force an

---

91   U.S. Department of the Interior, National Park Service, National Historic Landmark File, Office of Cultural Resource Management, Mid-Atlantic Region, U. S. Custom House, Philadelphia, PA., "Peggy Stewart House."

92   Park-Bernet Galleries, Inc., 980 Madison Ave., N.Y., N.Y. Sale number 2569, auction of May 16, 1967. P. 46, Lot 57, Thomas Stone letter to Walter Stone, 13 April 1783.

into Anne Arundel County court with a bill of complaint to force an heir of Daniel of St. Thomas Jenifer (died 1790) to pay monies still owed the estate of Thomas Stone. In the bill of complaint, having to do primarily with Stone's investment in the Baltimore Iron Works, Michael Jenifer mentions that Stone had purchased from his uncle

> certain lots and houses in the City of Annapolis and
> on or about the 30th day of May 1783 the said
> Jenifer passed his bond of conveyance to the said
> Stone for the conveyance of the same . . . And the
> said Thomas Stone on the said 30th day of May
> 1783 passed his bond to the said Jenifer for the sum
> of 2,250 pounds current money.

Apparently the difference between the 4,500 pounds purchase price and the 2,250 represented a debt Jenifer owed Stone. [93]

During the five-year period between Walter's going to Philadelphia and Thomas Stone's death there was frequent communication between the two on both personal and business matters. On May 20, 1783, Thomas, writing from Port Tobacco, tells Walter, already dissatisfied with his government job, that their uncle Daniel in Annapolis, the Intendant, has an opening for a clerk that pays 75 pounds a year, a rather generous clerical salary for the time. On July 3, 1783, Walter wrote to his uncle, turning down the job offer while at the same time indicating that his future in the government did not seem bright. The closing of this letter reflects the type of relationship that existed between Walter and his sophisticated, widely respected, wealthy uncle

> I am, dear sir, with great respect and esteem, your
> friend and humble servant, W. Stone. [94]

Between 1783 and 1787 Stone kept his law practice candle burning at two ends -- Port Tobacco and Annapolis. At the same time he tried to continue his involvement in politics. Things

---

93   Archives of Maryland, Maryland Hall of Records, Annapolis, MD.,
Chancery Court papers, Nr. 4818, Daniel of St. Thomas Jennifer [sic], 30
May 1783. Hereinafter, *C. C. Chancery Court.*

94   *LC-Stone Family, op.cit.*

sometimes went rather badly. At Habre de Venture Stone wrote on February 25, 1784, to William Paca, Governor of Maryland, apologizing for his failure to attend sessions of Congress in Annapolis. Stone said in his letter

> *It has given me very great pain that I have not been able to attend congress* [sitting in Annapolis] *in the course of the winter, but such has been the conditions of the weather that since my health has been restored it has not been practicable to travel in a carriage and I cannot ride any distance on horseback* [winter road conditions in Charles County were deplorable until well into the 20th Century] . . . *You may however be assured, sir, that both duty and inclination will lead me to Annapolis as soon as I can get there and in the meantime I hope my colleagues will keep the State represented*.

The matter of State representation in Congress was always serious. On occasion only three or four States out of the thirteen would be represented. [95] The record of attendance during the Annapolis sessions was especially dismal.

With respect to his business affairs things were disquieting. In the *Maryland Gazette* dated November 4, 1784, appeared the following notice

> *To Be Sold on Monday, the 8th day of November next, at the subscriber's mill, near Port Tobacco Town, in Charles County, Md., a number of valuable slaves, men, women and children; also horses, cattle, sheep and plantation utensils. Five years credit will be given for the purchase money, interest thereon being annually paid.   T. Stone*

Surely this advertisement indicated Stone's desperate need to convert property to money at this time.

---

95 David McNeely Stauffer autograph collection of the "Signers of the Declaration of Independence", 1876-1890, added to and printed by John Pierpont Morgan. Presented to Library of Congress, Washington, D.C. November 19, 1912.

By 1785 the John H. Stone Co. mercantile business had been established in Port Tobacco, managed by Walter but financed primarily by brother John Hoskins who lived permanently in Annapolis after his government military service. It may have been located in the large Thomas How Ridgate warehouse-residence, which still stands on the north side of the square in old Port Tobacco. The Stone Company dealt primarily with buying, selling and shipping tobacco. But apparently other kinds of merchandise were handled as well. On January 24, 1785, John Hoskins wrote to Walter (always addressed by family members as

Dear Watty [asking him to] ... *send up all the hair seating or chair bottom cloth with invoice ...* [96]

Maryland's third State House as it appeared during most of Stone's service in the State government. It is now the oldest state capitol in service in the United States.

---

[96] *LC-Stone Family, op.cit.*

A Lawyer's Lawyer

Stone was for years a highly respected peer of several pre-eminent barristers and judges holding high stations in Maryland's legal systems. The Carrolls, Thomas Johnson, Samuel Chase and William Paca may have been impressed by Stone's handling of Governor Eden's Anglican Church poll tax case in 1774. In this affair Stone defended the old, bitterly resented taxes against defense attorneys T. Johnson, S. Chase and W. Paca – all later to be colleagues in the Continental Congress. The juridical melee involved a recalcitrant member of the Maryland Assembly who refused to pay for supporting the State Church of Great Britain. [97]

A letter of December 7, 1775 from Stone to the Maryland Convention advised that

> *All business* [of the Convention] *was dispatched in Orderly, effective fashion and no body of men anywhere seemed better prepared for independence and self-government than the representatives of Maryland assembled in this extra-legal body.*

This "extra-legal" body governed Maryland between the exit of Sir Robert Eden and the First Constitution government of Maryland that placed first governor Thomas Johnson in the State's highest political post in early 1777. The Convention set in place three important commissions (Stone served on two) with directions to get Maryland on an effective wartime footing to counter incursions planned by the Crown.

In February 1776 Maryland delegate to Congress Robert Alexander implored the State Convention at Annapolis to send to Congress quickly as possible absent delegates Thomas Stone and Thomas Johnson to strengthen the Maryland contingent. Two of the appointed members, Chase and Rogers, could not attend. And Alexander's non-attendance future seemed precarious because of some personal business demands away from Philadelphia. Alexander promised to remain in Congress until properly relieved

---

97   E.C. Burnett, *Letters of Members of the Continental Congress*, VII. Hereinafter, *Letters of Members.*

by other delegates. [98]

On July 12, 1776, still thrilled by the amazing and potent document of July 4th, Stone wrote to the Council of Safety (executive arm of the State Convention)

> *. . . May God send victory to the arm lifted in support of righteousness, virtue and Freedom, and crush even to destruction the power which wantonly would trample on the rights of mankind . . . our province is now unrepresented although matters of the last consequence are coming on. I pray one of the Delegates* [of Maryland] *may be desired to attend* – [the Congress in Philadelphia]. *Mr. Paca is out* [not in attendance] *which occasions me alone to address you.*

So, here we have only Thomas Stone speaking for Maryland in Philadelphia late in July 1776 when much was having to be put into place politically, militarily and economically in support of the total Colonial posture being devised to confront the then awesome military and industrial capabilities of Great Britain. At this very same time Thomas Stone was laboring diligently under the leadership of John Dickinson to draft a constitutional type instrument which would, it was hoped, be the binding force of a new central government. What an overpowering responsibility for this one humble, tired man. The usual appellation of reluctant rebel, super conservative, pro-accommodation Colonial simply does not square with Stone's contribution and public statements during the July 1776 days immediately following our Declaration of Independence.

The Philadelphia responsibilities were debilitating and took a toll on Stone's fragile constitution. On September 9, 1776 Stone wrote to the Council in Annapolis that

> *. . . Mr. Chase and Paca left this place on Sunday and I shall set out on Thursday if my state of body will permit, tho this I much doubt being at present much* [in]*disposed.*

---

98 *Archives of Maryland*, Vol. XI, p.190.

Then by letter of December 12, 1776 the Council of Safety informed Stone that Mr. Carroll the barrister had requested the Council to ask Stone to remain in the Congress at Philadelphia as soon as

> *. . . your private concerns will permit, and we should be glad that you may have it in your power to gratify him.*

This request by one of Maryland's most prestigious and wealthy barristers, perhaps the best educated, most patriotic promoter of revolution, speaks volumes in support of Thomas Stone's reputation. This respect for Stone doubtless stemmed from an appreciation by Carroll of Stone's record in Congress as one of Maryland's leading advocates of independence and all-out opposition to Crown control of Americans of all thirteen colonies. [99]

A significant measure of the esteem in which Stone's peers held him at this time is what Maryland barrister and delegate Charles Carroll said about him in a letter to his father dated May 17, 1778:

> *. . . I have engaged Mr. [James] Wilson, an eminent lawyer of Pennsylvania who has lately removed into Maryland[100]. . . . I have also engaged Stone in my law business so that I think I have secured the two best lawyers that practice in our courts of law . . .*
> [101]

---

99   Archives of Maryland, Maryland Hall of Records, Letter of December 12, 1776 from Council of Safety for Maryland to Thomas Stone, p. 524.

100   *The World Book Encyclopedia*, (Chicago-London-Rome-Sydney-Toronto: Field Enterprise Educational Corporation, 1968), Vol. 20, p. 267. To place the Hon. James Wilson on the same professional step as Thomas Stone is an appropriate measure of each of these figures in the late 18th Century annals of American jurisprudence. Wilson, an associate justice of the Supreme Court of the United States, gave the first law lectures at the University of Pennsylvania where he was professor of law in the first law school in America, signed both the Declaration of Independence and the Constitution.

101   *Letters of Members, op.cit,*

This professional accolade came from one of the most suave, sophisticated barristers in America. His lengthy, formal, costly education in Europe helped produce a scholarly intellect that equaled the best in the Colonies. His admiration of Thomas Stone casts a new light on the man that greatly enhances his stature as a Founding Father.

Any hint of his being a "reluctant rebel" evaporated soon after July 4, 1776. During the next five years Stone's total support of the Revolution could not be denied by anyone familiar with the business of the Continental Congress in its promotion of the all-out effort to achieve a fair measure of victory. The collapse of Britain's will to subdue the Colonials was sparked by the unanticipated great Yorktown victory.

The Stone Private Law Practice

Stone's work in public affairs appears not to have had a stultifying effect on his growing law practice. Little is known of his work in Frederick during 1766-1771. At one time he kept two practices going – at Frederick and in Charles County. He could not, of course, sever all ties at once with Frederick and jump into a fully matured practice in southern Maryland. A substantial measure of the success of Stone's law work was in the final early 19th Century computation of his financial worth. The figures show clearly that Stone's law work and business acumen had taken him to an envied, substantial level of prosperity before his death.

One of Stone's early cases at Port Tobacco had to do with a difficult property settlement matter involving Mrs. Jeremiah Townly Chase whose husband had been an eminent judge in Annapolis. Their friendship developed when they were active debaters in the Forensic Club. In a June 16, 1770 letter Stone mentions going back to Frederick for a fortnight, and that on his return he will

> . . . *adjust her affairs with you in a manner that will*
> *require little time to ascertain the real balance due*
> *you – this person is very willing to pay and it will*
> *be a much more speedy and less expensive method*
> *than a Chancery suit* . . .

This letter reveals a bit of Stone in the early years of law practice. His writing is straightforward, very concise, and the penmanship is easily read even today.[102]

On June 14, 1771 Stone drafted a letter to gentlemen in Annapolis who were seeking settlement of their claims against Mrs. J. T. Chase, now living in Charles County. Stone suggests that the Annapolis people come to the county to visit Mrs. Chase

> *If you and the Doctor* [Stevenson] *could attend her*
> *in Charles County she would be much obliged and*
> *would settle the accounts to those articles on which*
> *you probably will differ* . . . *she has been uneasy to*
> *conclude this business long and would do anything*

---

102 MHS, *op. cit.*, MS 406.

to effect it. [103]

All quite clear and logical in the light of such lawyer labors yesterday and today.

On July 8, 1771 at Port Tobacco Stone again wrote Mrs. Chase about a lawsuit related to the claim of a Doctor Stevenson

> *... I have yours of the 29th of June and am very sorry to be informed of Doct. Stevenson's unfriendly disposition toward you, and unfeeling neglect of the very sacred trust reposed in him by your father. I did not suppose he or almost any man could be so cursed with such principles as to prevent an amicable settlement between relations so easily to be made, and thereby involve them in a tedious and expensive lawsuit, which must unavoidably produce trouble and inconvenience to all.* [104]

In a bit of a change of pace on June 29, 1781 Stone was involved in preparing a memorandum of agreement for a partnership that was to be part of a joint international trade arrangement involving the United States and a business house in Nantes, France. The memorandum had as its principals a Charles Wallace and John Muir of Maryland and Joshua Johnson of Nantes. Johnson was a brother of Governor Thomas Johnson. Stone signed this document as a witness for Wallace and Muir. The witness for Joshua Johnson was his attorney William Paca. [105]

An unusual legal item of Stone's was his letter of August 1782 to the Goose Creek (Quaker) Monthly Meeting, possibly the one located near Leesburg, Virginia. Stone wrote in response to

---

103 *MHS, op.cit.* MS 1303.

104 *MHS, op.cit.* Letter Thomas Stone to Mrs. J. T. Chase relative to the claim by Dr. Stevenson against the estate of Mrs. Chase's father. As with the other messages to the Chase family Stone was very candid and expressed himself in no-nonsense, clear English that would even today do credit to the best among our lawyer community.

105 Harvard University, the Houghton Library, Cambridge, MA.

1903 photograph of the south appendage, often called the Thomas Stone Law Office. It is doubtful that he ever saw it here. It may be one of the tenements on Habre de Venture cited in Daniel Jenifer's March 1769 advertisement in the *Maryland Gazette*.　　　　William Miller collection, Library of Congress

some uncomplimentary words by the Meeting that

> *The undersigned, without pretending to any*
> *exemption - from error, apprehends that his*
> *disavowment by Goose Creek Monthly Meeting has*
> *been partly if not wholly owing to an entire*
> *misconception of motives, and that even his conduct*
> *has been misrepresented, and believing that justice*
> *requires a disclosure of real facts without any*
> *partiality, hereby gives notice to said Meeting of his*
> *intention to appeal to the quarterly meeting.* [106]

On January 11, 1785 Thomas Stone as a member of the
Continental Congress wrote a lengthy brief to the Maryland
Assembly about the Captain Carbury affair. The facts of this matter
today seem beyond our comprehension. Captain Henry Carbury
had been arrested aboard his ship in Annapolis harbor. Perhaps the
arrest had to do with violations of the nation's export and import
laws. Stone was a member of the Congressional committee
responsible for such things. The Carbury arrest was reported to
Congress in an incorrect way. Stone addressed a letter to the
Maryland Assembly giving them new facts in the Carbury case that
had not reached Congress.

In a rather long seven-page document Stone concluded that
papers relating to the Carbury case got lost in Congress

> *. . . but S. F. Chase* [a Maryland Delegate]
> *recollects that the case is as I have stated it –*
> *Holding myself responsible to the General Assembly*
> *for my conduct in Congress I should with clear*
> [conscience?] *submit to their determination upon*
> *the part I ____ in this affair in which if I have erred*
> *I trust the Legislature will do me the justice to*
> *believe that I was not influenced by a desire to*
> *injure or oppress an individual, but was governed*
> *by principles which appeared to me to be just in*
> *discharge of what I esteemed my duty as a Citizen*
> *and Delegate of Maryland* [in the Congress].

---

106   The Huntington Library, San Marino, CA.

113

I am Gentlemen, Your
most obedient servant
T. Stone

Stone's written statements in the Carbury arrest case reveal something about the character of the man. Down across the passage of over two centuries his words reflect humility, honesty and a direct, plain presentation of facts as they were found, interpreted and described by one of America's ablest lawyers in late 18th Century. He now represented his native State in the Congress under the Articles of Confederation. [107]

Old Maryland Assembly Senate chamber (rear view). Scene familiar to Stone for eight years.

---

107 *Fogg, op.cit.* Letter Thomas Stone to the Assembly of Maryland, January 11, 1785.

A Tragic Finale

Stone was still a member of the Senate of Maryland the year he died. He was not active in the Assembly most of the year, not at all after his wife's death. Apparently, his wife's health deteriorated rapidly during 1787 and she died in Annapolis at the Peggy Stewart house June 3, 1787. She was interred at Habre de Venture. Contemporaries of Thomas Stone seem to agree that his wife's death was a shock his now frail constitution could not overcome. He left Annapolis and returned to Charles County when Margaret died. He had not been well for at least five years, as indicated in the correspondence between him and his brothers during that period. Certainly the continuous, very demanding public service of the previous twelve years and the attendant physical discomforts and mental requirements were exhausting.

Many years later Stone's two daughters and their husbands gave testimony, November 30, 1808, in Charles County court, probably in connection with the long-lasting lawsuit against the Jenifer estate. They described how difficult life had been at Habre de Venture with so many of their father's brothers and sisters living there on and off

> during the vicissitudes and disasters of the
> Revolutionary War when his distressed and
> struggling country claimed and enjoyed his
> services. [108]

On October 5, 1787, while in Alexandria waiting for a ship to take him on an ocean voyage prescribed by doctors and friends for his health, Thomas Stone died suddenly. The *Virginia Journal and Alexandria Advertiser* for October 11, 1787, advised its readers that

> *On the morning of the 5th instant departed this life
> in this place the Honorable Thomas Stone, Esq., a
> member of the Senate of Maryland, a man in whose
> character were combined the domestic virtues of
> private life and the more eminent talents of the
> statesman and legislator. His singular assiduity*

---

108   *C. C. Chancery Court, op.cit.*   Papers #4647 dated November 30, 1808.

and integrity, both as a professional man and in the several distinguishing and important offices of public trust wherein he hath been placed by his country, had long since gained him the universal confidence, gratitude and applause of his fellow citizens. His loss will be felt by his country -- to his family and friends it is irreparable.

Oddly, the *Maryland Gazette* in Annapolis never came close to expressing such acclaim and remorse over the death of Thomas Stone. Its sparse bare-bone comment appeared in the *Maryland Gazette* for January 10, 1788, as follows

Stone, Thomas, late of Annap., dec.; M.J.Stone, and G.R.Brown, execs.

Even the well-known Glassford & Company's records for stores in Colchester, Virginia and Port Tobacco, Maryland marked Thomas Stone's death with laudatory comments of great respect. An agent of Glassford wrote on October 12, 1787 to a southern Maryland friend that

. . . the only thing new here at present is the death of your great friend and acquaintance, Thomas Stone, Esq., attorney at law. It happened at Alexandria about eight days ago where he had gone to embark on board a vessel for the West Indies, his friends expecting a change of Climate and objects would better his health of body and mind. His daughters are to live with Dr. [Gustavus Richard of Rose Hill] Brown. [109]

Shortly before he died Stone wrote a letter to his son Frederick, then at Princeton University, that reveals a great deal about his character

My dear Frederick: I am now in a weak state, about to travel, and probably shall not see you more. Let me intreat you to attend to the following advice, which I leave you as a legacy; keep and read it, and

---

109   Edith Moore Sprouse, *Colchester: Colonial Port on the Potomac,* Fairfax, Virginia, March 1975. Glassford & Co. records, 1753-1834, 288 vols., Vol. #123, p. 121.

resort to it. In the first place, do your duty to God
in spirit and in truth, always considering Him as
your best protector, and doing all things to please
Him . . . Think more of your soul's health and the
next world than of this, and never do wrong on any
account . . . Seek the company of sober, virtuous
and good people . . . Seek to do all the good you
can, remembering that there is no happiness equal
to that which good actions accord . . . Take care not
to be seduced by the professions of any person to do
what your heart tells you is wrong, for on self-
approbation all happiness depends . . . Let your aim
in life be to attain the goodness rather than
greatness among men: The former is solid, the
latter all vanity, and often leads to ruin . . . This I
speak from experience . . . I commend you to
Heaven's protection. May God of His infinite
mercy protect you and lead you to happiness in this
world and the next is the most fervent prayer of
your loving Father. [110]

Stone's letter to his son certainly appears to have been a
goodbye message from one not planning to return. His will was
written a few weeks after Mrs. Stone's death. He directed in the
first few lines that he be buried at Habre de Venture next to his wife
according to rites of the Protestant Church. He had been raised as
an Anglican and probably attended the Episcopal church at
Nanjemoy (old Durham) in his youth. During Stone's last years at
Habre de Venture it seems quite certain he attended services at
Christ Church of Port Tobacco Parish. His will left the bulk of his
real estate to Frederick. However, the daughters were generously
provided for. In addition to each receiving 2,000 pounds "current
money" they were allowed to continue living at Habre de Venture
until married, supported by their inheritance income. [111] Michael J.

---

110   *Scharf, op.cit.*

111   Thomas Stone will, Liber AH7, ff. 459-463, undated, with codicil dated
July 20, 1787. The entire document was certified by the Charles County

Stone was appointed Frederick's guardian, which responsibility must have grieved him more than once since Frederick Stone was not a model student at the College of New Jersey (Princeton), where he received his A. B. degree in 1791. He had acted in concert with fellow students during mischievous escapades on campus – only a high-spirited aristocratic youth. [112]

When Thomas Stone died he owned about 3,000 acres in Charles County, a town house and four adjoining lots in Annapolis, a valuable one-fourth of one-tenth share of the Baltimore Iron Works, and eight years remaining on a leased twenty acres of mill land in Charles County on Port Tobacco Creek. Stone's total worth was not known for some time after his death. By 1798 a total of 4,189 pounds had been added to his estate from collection of debts and sales of property. In 1809 fifteen slaves with a total value of $3,090 were given to the Stone estate in partial settlement of Daniel of St. Thomas Jenifer's debt to his nephew. Including the valuations placed on Habre de Venture and Plenty during efforts to secure valid titles to both properties, $14,100 was added to the Stone estate. This sum added to the 1798 and 1809 estate income added up to Stone having been a very wealthy man when he died. This was a remarkable achievement for a Poynton Manor country boy who went to Annapolis about 1762 to begin a glittering, grand new life among prominent barristers and others moving easily among the Capital's high society. Upon his death Stone owned at least twenty-five slaves. He had a library of 530 law books, 258 other bound volumes and 121 unbound pamphlets. [113] Stone's law library was appraised in March 1788 at a little more than 454 pounds, an indication of a valuable collection in that time. [114]

Register of Wills December 10, 1787.

112   *Princetonians:* Princeton University, Firestone Library, Princeton, NJ, *A Biographical Dictionary* MS.

113   *MHR Biographical Dictionary, op. cit.* Vol. 2.

114   Alan F. Day dissertation, *A Social Study of Lawyers in Maryland 1660-1775.* Edinburgh, 1976. Maryland State Archives, Maryland Hall of Records, Annapolis, Md. pp. 1117-1120.

A simple epitaph remains easily read on Stone's austere grave at Habre de Venture

Son of David and Elizabeth Stone departed this life on the 5th of Oct. 1787 Aged 44 years The archives of Maryland will show the offices of trust he has held. He was an able and faithful lawyer, a wise and virtuous Patriot, an honest and good man.

In an almost postscript way, Stone's Virginia friend-statesman, Richard Henry Lee, mentioned Stone in respectful tribute in a letter to George Mason late in 1787. Virginia often placed recognition and credit for outstanding Stone accomplishments to a degree seldom matched by Maryland. In a letter dated October 1, 1787 by Richard Henry Lee to George Mason, Lee commented:

You are well acquainted with Mr. Stone and others of influence in Maryland.

At this time the Southern States at the Constitutional Convention were struggling to slow a steamroller effort to word the new document in a way that could hurt the plantation economics of States south of the Potomac.

Lee hoped that Virginia with Maryland support might slow progress on drafting of the Constitution until the southern States could unite forcefully in having changes made that would assure a united State support the for the new government. Lee stated in his letter that if adopted the document as then written might lead to civil war . . . how incredibly prophetic. Who knows now what affect the cool and perceptive intellect of Stone may have had in the final draft of the Constitution of the United States. [115] Apparently Lee was not aware that Stone would take no part at the Constitutional Convention.

---

115 Kate Mason Rowland The Letters of Richard Henry Lee,, *The Life of George Mason*, II. 185. New York, NY, 1914.

The Letters of Richard Henry Lee

To [George Mason][116]

New York,
*   October 1st, 1787*

Dear Sir,
*   I have waited until now to answer your favor*
of September 10th from Philadelphia, that I might
inform you how the Convention plan of government
was entertained by Congress. Your prediction of
what would happen in Congress was exactly
verified. It was with us, as with you, this or
nothing; and this urged with a most extreme
intemperance. The greatness of the powers given,
and the multitude of places to be created produce a
coalition of monarchy men, military men,
aristocrats and drones, whose noise, impudence and
zeal exceeds all belief. Whilst the commercial
plunder of the South stimulates the rapacious
trader. In this state of things the patriot voice is
raised in vain for such changes and securities as
reason and experience prove to be necessary
against the encroachments of power upon the
indispensable rights of human nature. Upon due
consideration of the Constitution under which we
now act, some of us were clearly of opinion that the
Thirteenth Article of the Confederation precluded
us from giving an opinion concerning a plan
subversive of the present system, and eventually
forming a new Confederacy of nine instead of
thirteen States. The contrary doctrine was asserted
with great violence in expectation of the strong
majority with which they might send it forward

---

116 *Ibid.*

*under terms of much approbation. Having
procured an opinion that Congress was qualified to
consider, to amend, to approve or disapprove, the
next game was to determine that though a right to
amend existed, it would be highly inexpedient to
exercise that right, but merely to transmit it with
respectful marks of approbation. In this state of
things I availed myself of the right to amend, and
moved the amendments, a copy of which I send
herewith, and called the ayes and nays to fix them
on the journal. This greatly alarmed the majority
and vexed them extremely; for the **plan is to push
the business on with great dispatch, and with as
little opposition as possible,** that it may be adopted
before it has stood the test of **reflection and due
examination.** They found it most eligible at last to
transmit it merely, without approving or
disapproving, provided nothing but the transmission
should appear on the journal. This compromise
was settled and they took the opportunity of
inserting the word unanimously, which applies only
to simple transmission, hoping to have it mistaken
for an unanimous approbation of the thing. It
states that Congress having received the
Constitution unanimously transmit it, &c. It is
certain that no approbation was given. This
Constitution has a great many excellent regulations
in it, and if it could be reasonably amended would
be a fine system. As it is, I think 'tis past doubt,
that if it should be established, either a tyranny will
result from it, **or it will be prevented by a civil war.**
I am clearly of opinion with you that it should be
sent back with amendments reasonable, and assent
to it withheld until such amendments are admitted.
**You are well acquainted with Mr. Stone and
others of influence in Maryland.***

Burial ground at Habre de Venture. Three generations of the family are buried here. First was Margaret in June 1787 and next was Thomas in October 1787. They rest side by side with Thomas next to the wrought iron fence (below).   Photo by John M. Wearmouth

Part III
Crossing the "T's"
Thomas and Thomas

Those who have read Edward S. Delaplaine's The Life of
Thomas Johnson, published in 1927, should have a fundamental
understanding about the Thomas Johnson-Thomas Stone
contribution to the founding of the State of Maryland and our
Nation. [117] During 1775, 1776 and again in 1781, these two
prominent lawyers worked closely and harmoniously to achieve
advantage for Americans and put a democratic nation and society
into place. At about the time of its publication Johnson was praised
by Maryland Governor Albert C. Ritchie who stated: "Biographical
justice has not been done many of the great men of Maryland."
Without any apparent intention to add laurels to the name of
Thomas Stone, Judge Delaplaine, by simply describing Johnson's
Revolutionary War contributions, had placed Stone in a very
positive and notable light as a major player in the Colonial
deliberations and actions that led to a complete rupture of political
ties to Great Britain. The Governor's 1927 words regarding
Johnson certainly had equal application to Stone, the country
gentleman from Charles County, Maryland.

The Brig *Peggy Stewart*, beached and burning at Windmill Point, Annapolis Harbor October 19, 1774. Her destroyed taxable tea cargo did not raise a ha'penny for the Crown.

---

117 Edward S. Delaplaine, *The Life of Thomas Johnson*, 1927, New York.
Hereinafter, *Delaplaine, Johnson.*

Thomas Johnson -
Maryland's First Elected Governor

Like Stone, Johnson was sent by his family from their home in Calvert County to Annapolis to read the law. Under mentor Stephen Bordley's tutorship, Johnson gained as fine an education in the law as was available anywhere in the Colonies. He first served on the Maryland committee for dealing with consequences of the 1765 Stamp Act. In 1768 he helped draft a complaint to the King about acts of Parliament imposing duties on the Colonies for raising revenue -- **taxation without representation**. In 1773 Johnson was chosen to serve on Maryland's Committee of Correspondence and Enquery. In 1774 he was elected to the Convention of Maryland and to the First Continental Congress. In the Second Continental Congress he recommended that Washington be appointed Commander-in-Chief of the Continental Army -- this nomination was approved. In August 1775 he became a member of Maryland's Council of Safety. In January 1776 the Maryland Convention elected Johnson to be senior Brigadier General of Maryland militia. Under Maryland's First Constitution he was elected February 13, 1777 as the State's first governor.[118] This ever so illustrious patriot served as a magnificent role model for his young friend Thomas Stone.

Stone studied at the Annapolis law office of Johnson for about five years – 1762-1766. The Thomases by 1768 knew each other well in a relationship of mentor-student as well as law practice associates. Why Stone joined the Thomas Johnson firm can only be a matter of conjecture. But Stone's illustrious uncle, Daniel of St. Thomas Jenifer, knew Annapolis people of prominence, including well-founded, successful gentlemen of the Bar. Stone's mother was a sister of Jenifer. The Thomases' mutual respect stood them and this nation in good stead until Stone's death in 1787.

Marylander Edward S. Delaplaine's *Johnson*, presents a larger than life detailed description of Johnson as a Revolutionary War period patriot unknown to most Americans today. His legacy stems from a contribution to the Revolutionary War cause perhaps

---

118 Maryland House of Delegates Journal, February session 1777, pp. 50-51.

Thomas Johnson served under Maryland's Constitution of 1776 when for the first time the State ruled itself free of Crown overlordship. Its first elected governor Johnson held this office for two years. He, as Stone, had been sent from a Southern Maryland home to study under renowned barrister Stephen Bordley. Maryland State Archives

unsurpassed by any other notable figure who forged critical, unbreakable links in the chain of events that produced the most earthshaking political upheaval in the history of Western Society. Johnson may be best known now as having been Maryland's first governor under the first State constitution following the Declaration of Independence. His avid, uncompromising fight for independence began as a member of the First Continental Congress that convened early in September 1774 at Philadelphia. Johnson's dissatisfaction with Crown arrogance and arbitrary taxation of the Colonies began with the lengthy, contentious efforts of the Maryland Assembly to set equitable fees allowed many Crown government officials who were part of the province's tobacco inspection system. He became deeply involved in this sticky matter in 1765, when it was discovered that many highly placed Proprietary officials were lining their pockets by charging unreasonably high fees in connection with tobacco inspection.

By the end of the First Continental Congress Johnson had earned the utmost respect of the most illustrious representatives of the other Colonies. He was seen by many as Maryland's most able member . . . one whose contributions were shaped by broad understanding of law, trade, finance, military and political matters. Thomas Stone's already long professional association with Johnson (about ten years) prepared the younger advocate and patriot for insightful and notable participation in the affairs of the Second Continental Congress. And Delaplaine's Johnson makes it clear that Stone was always a staunch supporter of Johnson in the Congress as both kept pace with the other Colonial leading rebels while relations with King and Ministry in London worsened to the point where reconciliation was no longer an option.

The following chronology of events in 1775 and 1776 illustrates when and how Stone's weight influenced the political course of Colonial direction toward the finalization of wording in the July 2, 1776 Declaration announced two days later to expectant citizens of a new nation. In less than a century this Philadelphia-forged instrument would make its influence felt around the world in degrees and ways that would have astounded both Johnson and Stone. Within the decade ushered in by Yorktown and the Treaty of Paris the Parisian "rabble" at the French Revolution barricades were heartened by what Americans in rebellion had achieved against a mightier empire.

Thomas Stone's almost indelible, conservative reputation for several years paralleled the stance of Thomas Johnson. In the First Continental Congress he was thought somewhat conservative about taking paths toward revolution. However, in 1774 Johnson was appointed to a Committee of Correspondence soon after news of the Boston Port Bill reached Maryland. This committee was asked to plan for a Congress that would bring representatives from each Colony together to decide what had to be done for securing the rights of freemen.

When Thomas Stone was seated for the Second Continental Congress the Annapolis directions to the Maryland delegates probably squared with Johnson's views during the earlier Congress . . . all Maryland delegates were very ill at ease now about any all-out drive for independence. John Adams stated in his diary that

> . . . *Johnson had a clear, cool head . . . His passions and imagination don't appear enough for an orator . . . his reason and penetration appear, but not his rhetoric.*

Adams also noted that Johnson was the most frequent Maryland speaker in the First Congress as he fought suggested radical measures that may have destroyed reconciliation prospects. But, Adams states, he and his State "joined our camp" and eventually provided support of measures to achieve separation from the Crown. [119] These actions of Thomas Johnson in the First Continental Congress closely paralleled those of his close friend Thomas Stone in the Second Continental Congress. For many years historians have suggested that Stone's written word was far more effective than his oral delivery--certainly, he was nowhere near being a Patrick Henry or Richard Henry Lee. But when Stone spoke people who knew him respected his intellect, mature wisdom and deep patriotic inclinations. And they listened to him carefully, no doubt.

John Quincy Adams and Charles Francis Adams (in editing

---

119 *Adams Papers, Works of John Adams,* C. F. Adams, Ed., Vol. II, p.506

works of John Adams) refer to Thomas Johnson, along with John Dickinson, Caesar Rodney and several others of their caliber as having

> *sincerity of purpose and cautious judgment as*
> *well as practical capacity, which would not have*
> *discredited the most experienced statesmen of their*
> *day.*

These men had been leading lights in the First Continental Congress in which Stone was not a member. Had he been, the editors Adams quite likely would have included the name of Thomas Stone because their crediting of those named included a most fitting **description of the strengths brought to bear by Stone in the Second Continental Congress and in Maryland Assembly deliberations right through 1781.**

When the Second Continental Congress convened in Philadelphia in May 1775 **Thomas Stone of Charles County joined the First Continental Congress contingent that had included Samuel Chase, William Paca, John Hall, and Matthew Tilghman.** That young lawyer Stone, something of a down-State rustic from old Port Tobacco, was considered in Annapolis a worthy addition to such an illustrious group leaves little more to be said by way of adding luster to the patriotism, integrity, intellect and strength of character of Thomas, probably one of the most illustrious Marylanders of all times.

June 1775 Continental Congress Declaration to be published by **General George Washington in New England** . . . a Petition to the King, which was signed by Colonial representatives **including Thomas Stone for Maryland**. This petition explained to the Ministry and Parliament the position of the American Colonies with respect to the outstanding major differences between Crown and its North American citizens.

After dispatching Royal Governor Sir Robert Eden in 1775, the Maryland Convention opened in July of this year

> *. . . It considered ways and means of putting this*
> *Province into the best state of defense*

A committee was appointed to make plans for such a posture . . . **Thomas Stone** was a member of this body with Thomas Johnson, Matthew Tilghman, William Paca, Samuel Chase, Robert

Goldsborough, Charles Carroll of Carrollton, Charles Carroll, barrister, and James Hollyday . . . **all Marylanders known to be devoted to the "Common Cause."** On August 9 the Committee presented a powerful resolution to the State Convention stating that

> *The long premeditated, and now avowed, design of*
> *the British Government to raise a revenue from the*
> *property of the Colonists without their consent, on*
> *the gift, grant and disposition of the Commons of*
> *Great Britain: The arbitrary and vindictive statutes*
> *passed under color of punishing a riot, to subdue by*
> *force and by famine the Massachusetts Bay Colony.*

Thomas Stone was appointed a member from the Western Shore on the new Maryland Council of Safety, which assembled August 10, 1775 for the first time under the new State Government that succeeded the Colonial establishment led by Sir Robert Eden. Stone's politically influential and experienced uncle, Daniel of St. Thomas Jenifer, also served on this Council. So the far southern precincts of the State were well represented in the new State governing machinery.

On October 6, 1775 Stone joined his friend and mentor Thomas Johnson in a broad Congressional effort to encourage Virginians to depose their despised Colonial Governor, Lord Dunmore (John Murray). Dunmore had strong naval forces active in the mouth of the James River. He was now in a tactical and strategic position to damage Maryland as well as Virginia. Dunmore's powerful flotilla could inflict havoc on the coastal settlements of both Virginia and Maryland. So, here we have our "reluctant rebel" Stone siding with treason and sedition against the Crown almost a year before Independence was declared. And the gravity of this action must be measured in the light of Virginia's standing among Britain's North American Colonies. She had been the jewel in the crown since the early 17th Century. Probably Stone agreed when Johnson proclaimed before the Continental Congress that

> . . . *Maryland does not regard the connection with*
> *Great Britain as the first good.*

And Stone echoed Johnson's words by suggesting that the Congress indicate to Virginia that anything that colony might do to halt Dunmore's coastal depredations would meet with Maryland approval. The Virginia Council of Safety was so informed. However, Dunmore continued a potent threat until mid-1776. [120]

This early effort by Thomas Stone to destroy Colonial power in what was then perhaps the wealthiest and largest of the Colonies surely must mark him as one of the early firebrands in support of revolution. He has never been viewed by historians in this light. The same old measures of his role in the Second Continental Congress have been repeated endlessly for years. For anyone to suggest that Stone was really cautious, a friend of the King, or afraid to commit to total revolution, simply does not stand up to close scrutiny. Samuel Adams and John Adams, two of New England's most dynamic revolutionaries, contributed no more than Thomas Stone and Thomas Johnson in their efforts to strike a major blow for independence--beginning with the Colony of Virginia in October 1775.

At this time Maryland's new State Government . . . the Convention . . . and last Royal Governor were managing more or less successfully to pursue dual governing roles that allowed a considerable degree of mutual sufferance. This peculiar situation existed in great part because until just a few weeks before the Declaration of Independence was signed the Convention policy remained committed to a possibility of compromise. Any effort that might lead to reconciliation with the Crown was thought desirable by the Convention. During the previous year adherents of Independence had gained ever increasing strength, especially among the New England leaders. Until total evaporation of reconciliation hopes, Sir Robert Eden remained socially and politically acceptable to the most patriotic and distinguished members of the State Convention and the Council of Safety. The Council was directed by its President, Daniel of St. Thomas Jenifer, long the Maryland Intendant for the Crown and a strong advocate of compromise with Britain.

During the primary months of ambivalence in Maryland with respect to prospects for reconciliation, Thomas Johnson remained the most active and stalwart representative in Congress of the

---

120 *Delaplaine, Johnson, op.cit.*

Maryland Convention . . . even when he commanded the State Militia as a formidable additional critical duty. And during this period Johnson had no greater a supporter than Thomas Stone of Port Tobacco. Their deliberations in the Second Continental Congress were founded firmly on their loyalty to the Maryland Convention and its understanding about what courses of action would likely be most beneficial to the State over the long unfolding of American human experience in years to come.

The Johnson and Stone view of things was not cemented in stifling opinion and rhetoric. They yielded intelligently to the realism of developing events and attitudes. In October 1775 Johnson told the Congress that

> *. . . I see less and less prospect of a reconciliation*
> *every day; but I would not render it impossible.*

Other Maryland members of Congress also felt this way. **Late in April 1776** Thomas Stone in a letter to Jenifer wrote

> *I wish to conduct affairs so that a just and*
> *honorable reconciliation should take place, or that*
> *we should be pretty unanimous in a resolution to*
> *fight it out for independence . . . WE MUST TAKE*
> *CARE TO DO EVERYTHING WHICH IS*
> *NECESSARY FOR OUR SECURITY AND*
> *DEFENCE . . . WAR, ANYTHING IS*
> *PREFERABLE TO A SURRENDER OF OUR*
> *RIGHTS.*

These certainly cannot be the words of anyone not prepared to sever completely all relations with Great Britain . . . nor can they be understood to be any unreasonably conservative thoughts. They were simply expressions of a mind and a reflection of an allegiance to any highway into the future that might assure a well-founded promise for health, safety, dignity and prosperity of the new Nation that seemed on the threshold of birthing.

In January 1776 Thomas Stone in company with Matthew Tilghman, Thomas Johnson and James Hollyday had sanctioned Governor Eden's request to send a messenger to Britain with indications of Maryland's leaning toward hope for reconciliation. Sir Robert sent copies of recent resolutions of the Maryland Convention that exalted

*. . . the mildness and equity of the English
Constitution.”* [121]

While still desiring fair and honorable reconciliation with
Britain under mutually acceptable terms, realistic Marylanders
continued preparations for open conflict, including armed
confrontation. Even as Sir Robert's messenger traveled toward
New York to board ship for England, the chief of the province's
militia forces, Brigadier General Thomas Johnson, began war
preparations in central and western parts of the State . . . known as
"the Upper District." [122]

Since Johnson and Stone were nearly always in step with
respect to the Colonial cause it surely can be assumed now that
Stone supported General Johnson's work rallying the militia and
locating armaments and resources for producing military supplies.
By 1776 Stone and Johnson had long been compatriots and
professionals in the study and practice of the law . . . beginning with
Stone's arrival in Annapolis from his Charles County family home
on Nanjemoy Creek about 1762. Stone was accepted to "read law"
in the relatively new law office of Thomas Johnson, Jr., then only
about thirty years old. Most assuredly, Stone could not in all of
the Colonies have understudied more capable and respected law
practitioners than those then in the Johnson law office in Annapolis.
When a fledgling lawyer, Stone began his law career in Frederick
about 1766 doubtless because Johnson himself had a deep and
growing interest in central and western regions of the Province.
Four of Johnson's brothers already were established as
professionals and businessmen in this section of Maryland. And
two of them had studied with Johnson in Annapolis and Stone must
have known them there. Thomas Johnson himself had been
admitted to the Bar of Frederick County in 1760. Stone's law
practice in his native Charles County did not begin until 1770. [123]

It took the courage and passionate oratory of a Virginia

---

121   *Maryland Archives*, Vol. XI, p. 109.

122   *Ibid*, p. 120.

123   *Delaplaine, Johnson, op.cit.* PP. 13-18.

delegate to spark the dissolution of reconciliation sentiments. On June 7, 1776, Richard Henry Lee advanced his long respected, breathtaking resolution to Congress that

The United States are, and of right ought to be, free

- - - and as soon as possible. Of course, exciting debate followed but on June 10 the members voted to put off final action until July 1. This gave Maryland members breathing time to contact the Council of Safety and suggest convening the Convention to study the new slant of things in Philadelphia . . . and the apparent fast general drifting away from thoughts of reconciliation. Members of Congress from other Colonies were likewise asking for revised marching instructions in case the Congress supported the Lee resolution when members reconvened in July. New York delegates were sitting under more severe constraints than most delegations, including the four Maryland representatives.

The patriots in Annapolis moved quickly. In fact, already feeling that reconciliation was now a quite moribund issue, the Maryland Convention on June 27 decided to contribute 3,400 troops to be the State's portion of the June 3 Congressional recommendation for establishment of a "Flying Camp" body of troops. [124]

Late in June 1776 the Maryland Convention at Annapolis almost unanimously determined that Maryland could no longer fight the much broadened turn toward actions leading to total independence. In the reconvened Second Continental Congress Maryland members were free to support the majority in any popular move toward independence. On June 28, 1776, only four days before the independence vote on July 2, the Convention resolved

That the instructions given by the Convention of December last [and renewed by the Convention in May] to the deputies of the Colony in Congress, be recalled, and the restrictions therein contained removed; that the deputies of this Colony attending in Congress, or a majority of them, or any three or more of them, be authorized and

---

124   *Maryland Archives*, Vol. XI, pp. 478, 490; *Proceedings of Conventions*, p. 166.

empowered to concur with the other United
Colonies, or a majority of them, in declaring the
United Colonies free and independent States...

And at long last Thomas Stone and his fellow members in
Congress sitting for Maryland were liberated from the binding
restraints set by Annapolis when reconciliation with the Crown
seemed possible and desirable.

For many years historians, including Maryland scholars,
have repeated the fallacious, obnoxious canard that Thomas Stone
of Habre de Venture at Port Tobacco signed the Declaration of
Independence quite reluctantly. It is totally unfair and unscholarly
to allow these views to continue. Somehow, down through many
decades, this understanding (more likely a lack of it) has resulted in
Stone being seen as something of a lukewarm, even reluctant
patriot, badgered and coaxed into becoming a Signer. In truth,
Thomas Stone worked hand in glove and in perfect step with the
entire Maryland delegation at the Second Continental Congress . . .
in strict compliance with the clear directions of the Maryland
Convention in Annapolis. Delaplaine in *Johnson* sheds a great deal
of light on this.

The joint efforts of Johnson and Stone in 1781 to ease
Maryland into ratifying the Articles of Confederation in and of
themselves should long ago have cast these two Greats as bright
and spectacular figures in both National and State history. After
the American victory at Saratoga late in 1777 the Colonials felt
they could soon expect help from France, but it simply didn't
materialize in any significant way. Lack of a forceful central
government chilled French ardor for actively supporting the new,
shaky nation. It still had no centralized political muscle worth being
held in international esteem -- in great part because Maryland had
refused to ratify the Articles, for over four years, along with a small
group of other States having no Crown charter rights to western
lands.

The Maryland Assembly in early 1781 made ratification a
very high priority matter. This came about because of a strongly
worded warning letter to Daniel of St. Thomas Jenifer from a close
friend. The writer, Chevalier de la Luzerne, was the French
Minister to the United States living in Philadelphia. He knew that

total ratification depended upon Maryland leadership.

The Chevalier hinted that Maryland's failure to ratify could have grave consequences for continuation of the France-U.S. Alliance. This somewhat oblique threat really was ignited by a January 5, 1781 letter to the French Minister from Daniel of St. Thomas Jenifer. This letter was in effect a plea for French naval assistance to help counter British naval power, which for several months had moved at will and in strength the length of the Bay and deeply into navigable tributaries. Luzerne's reply of January 10 included a suggestion, rather sharply worded, that Maryland herself should take measures to deal with Britain's naval power loose in waters that touched Maryland shores for hundreds of miles from the Head of Elk [north end of the Bay] nearly to Georgetown on the Potomac River.

The French Minister went on in the same letter, rather bluntly stating

> *We are led to hope, Gentlemen, that the winter will*
> *not come to an end without the accession*
> [ratification] *of your state to the confederation.*
> *This resolution is so fitting to endow with some*
> *energy the activities of the Thirteen States, to*
> *strengthen their union . . . that all good citizens can*
> *see only with satisfaction that the obstacles which*
> *have hitherto stood in the way of accession have*
> *been at last removed* [the western lands question].

The de la Luzerne letter was prepared without the knowledge of Louis XVI and Mr. Vergennes, the French Minister of Foreign Affairs. When finally receiving a copy of the letter Vergennes complimented de la Luzerne

> *You have grasped perfectly, Monsieur, the spirit of*
> *the King's policy, and his opinion as to the*
> *government of the United States . . . we have greatly*
> *applauded the step which you took to bring to an*
> *end the irresolution of the Marylanders . . .*

It seems clear now that the Maryland assembly vote to ratify was indeed an absolutely essential step toward the young nation's long-range independence assured by the Yorktown victory. And this was made possible by Maryland's ratification after a firm nudging by the new nation's only European ally of strength and stature. Maryland's Governor Thomas Sim Lee signed the legislation on February 2, 1781. [125]

Things in Annapolis now moved into high gear toward ratification. The two old friends -- Johnson in the House of Delegates and Stone (temporarily) chairing the Senate, united their efforts to bring about Maryland's ratification vote, giving the fledgling republic a viable central political authority for the first time. The Colonies hereby became "as one firm cemented body."

Now treating with one nation and a single central government France quickly acted to reinforce both sea and land forces in North America to supply the battered Colonials close-up, immediate assistance. French regulars under General Comte de Rochambeau began disembarking in Rhode Island the summer of 1780. Then, in 1781, after a long overland march to Yorktown in late summer and early fall, the united French and Americans knotted the lion's tail, thus ending the American Revolutionary War. Truly, then, the world seemed to all "turned upside down." Victory at Yorktown had its roots in the Johnson-Stone efforts to steer the Maryland Assembly toward immediate ratification early in 1781. This placed the new nation in a much stronger position to assure its continued independence from the feared, long revered, and powerful motherland. And all this is to the everlasting credit of the Thomases -- that in the morass of crises they engineered a remarkable political feat -- peacefully and expeditiously.

---

125 *Sioussat, Luzerne, op.cit.* PP. 392-394, 401-403, 405.

Part IV
The Signer's Domain

Thomas Stone's best known home was Habre de Venture from 1771-1783. The earliest reference to Habre de Venture (spelled Habberdeventure) is in the Charles County rent rolls for the late 17th century. These records indicate that Habre de Venture originally was only a 150-acre plantation in the West Port Tobacco Hundred. First surveyed March 16, 1682, for Thomas Barefoot, it joined properties called Simpson's Delight and Betty's Delight along its western and southern boundaries. In 1685 this tract was passed on to Thomas Barefoot's son, John. The name seems to have originated with the Barefoots although old records indicate that there was a property in 17th century Charles County named Hab Nab at a Venture, which may have been refined late in that century into Habre de Venture, the exact meaning of which remains obscure. [126] Beginning in 1695 the ancient Post Road from adjoining St. Mary's County to Philadelphia (by way of Piscataway) closely marked its eastern boundary. Under ownership of several planters from 1685 to 1770, the property grew steadily to reach the acreage bought by Stone in 1770.

In the later years of Thomas Stone's possession the greater Habre de Venture holdings were pushed far beyond the 1770 western bounds of the Hog Hole-Gambra Run line. Acreage of the plantation was expanded from 442 acres in 1770 to about 1,300 in 1787. Then, just before mid-19th century, a great contraction began. By 1880 the old estate had returned to a size and location amazingly close to the 1770 bounds. Today, under National Park Service ownership, at least three-quarters of the Habre de Venture boundaries follow closely those of a century ago.

On December 13, 1770, young lawyer Thomas Stone, then living in Frederick, Maryland, purchased from Daniel Jenifer (brother of Daniel of St. Thomas Jenifer)the recently patented 442 acres called Habberdeventure-Hanson's Plains Enlarged. The

---

126   Archives of Maryland, Maryland Hall of Records, Charles County Rent Roll, Liber 8, folio 322. Hereinafter *C. C. Rent Roll.*

property was just as surveyed by Theophilus Hanson three years earlier. The matter of dower rights was an important part of the transaction. Mary Hanson Jenifer had formerly (voluntarily, of course) relinquished dower rights to her inheritance before the justices of the Charles County court, as described at the bottom of the deed recorded by Stone March 20, 1771. It has long been said that the 400 pounds sterling paid by Stone for his property was part of a 1,000-pound dowry of his wife, Margaret, from her father, Charles County's generous and illustrious Gustavus Brown, M. D. He already had endowed eight other daughters who had married very well either at or above their perceived station in society. In any event, it is rather doubtful that Thomas Stone, married only about three years, with at least one child (son Frederick) and a not yet lucrative law practice on the Maryland frontier, could have accumulated so much sterling in about three years without Margaret's help. [127]

After 1771 and continuing well into 1787, the year he died, Thomas Stone remained very active in Charles County court matters and real estate transactions. Even before the Revolution began he held mortgages on at least four county properties other than Habre de Venture-connected lands. Such enterprise by county attorneys often represented major sources of income for practitioners of the law. The real estate involvement doubtless went hand in hand with Stone's growing Charles County law practice, each building upon the other. [128]

In 1785 Stone resurveyed eight tracts touching or lying close to the package he purchased in 1770. These were (with original survey dates): The Barefoot property, 150 acres, 1682; Hanson's Plains, Robert Hanson, 75 acres, 1725; Habbredeventure and Hanson's Plains Enlarged, Daniel Jenifer, 442 acres, 1768; Simpson's Delight, Alexander Simpson, 300 acres, 1664; Bridget's Delight, James Lenkins, 63 acres, 1660; Part of St. Nicholas, Ignatius Causin, 300 acres, 1664; Betty's Delight, Thomas Corker,

---

127 *C. C. Land Records, op.cit.* Liber S3, pp. 127, 130.

128 *Ibid.,* Liber S4, pp. 410, 412, 500, 509, 532, 539, 547, 550m, 700 and 710. Also, Liber V3, pp. 51, 66, 76, 80 and 205.

150 acres, 1671; and Prior's Beginning, Prior Theobald, 10 acres, 1767. The total of these properties were repatented for Stone in 1787 in one large consolidated holding. When he died October 5, 1787, he possessed a 1,077-acre greatly expanded Habre de Venture plantation. It still followed old boundaries very closely on the east side and along the easternmost lines of the north and south property limits. Many plats for the older Charles County property surveys have long been missing. Stone's 1785 survey plat seems to be one of them. However, the Habre de Venture holdings surveyed in 1830 by Thomas Perry, Charles County surveyor, must have come very close to reflecting the greater Habre de Venture bounds as they were when Thomas Stone died.[129]

Stone's will, undated but with codicil dated July 20, 1787, and probated December 10th of that year, leaves to his only son, Frederick, his large and most valuable land holdings in Charles County: Habre de Venture and the Plenty package, which included Addition to Mayday Enlarged and Moberly. The latter three properties were located east of Port Tobacco Run and just beyond the northern edge of the village of Port Tobacco. None of the Stone children had reached their majority when their father died and so could play no part in decisions about execution of his will by his brother, Michael Jenifer, and his brother-in-law, Dr. Gustavus Richard Brown of Rose Hill which adjoined Habre de Venture to the south. [130]

When Frederick died intestate of yellow fever early in September 1793 at Princeton, New Jersey, the ownership of the properties he had inherited devolved upon his younger sisters, Margaret and Mildred, jointly. This matter of "jointly" led to considerable trouble many years later. In 1821 the heirs of Margaret (who died in 1809) filed a bill of complaint in the Charles County court to try to gain legal possession of the Plenty lands patented to his daughters jointly in 1794 after their brother's death.

---

129 Archives of Maryland, Maryland Hall of Records, Annapolis, MD., *Patents & Tracts*, July 27, 1787, Liber IC B, folio 634.

130 Archives of Maryland, Maryland Hall of Records, Annapolis, MD. *Charles County Wills*, Liber AH#9, pp. 459, 460. Hereinafter, *C. C. Wills*.

The resulting proceedings dragged on through 1827. At that time the entire property had been awarded by the state to the sisters jointly by a patent dated 26 May 1794.

The patent did not delineate or describe with precision the lands and improvements of the Habre de Venture and Plenty tracts. Mildred (the younger sister) testified that the Plenty tract had long been considered the property of Margaret and her heirs. The girls agreed informally that Mildred would have Habre de Venture and Margaret Plenty plus May Day Enlarged and Moberly. The sisters, just into their majority, gave little thought to relative current market values of these properties.

Finally, in 1827, after many trips back and forth across the Potomac River, Margaret's heirs and their aunt, Mildred, at long last received satisfaction. In March that year the Charles County justices sitting as a Court of Equity established a commission of four prominent citizens to arbitrate and resolve the matter and to assign proper and legal ownership of Habre de Venture and the greater Plenty tract. One of the commissioners was Gustavus Brown, son of Dr. Gustavus Richard Brown, and related to all the principals involved, his aunt Margaret having been the wife of Thomas Stone. On August 4, 1827, the commissioners reported to the court that they had come to a solution. They proposed dividing the properties into two equal shares of like current value. Habre de Venture was found to contain 1,137 acres valued at $5.50 each for a total of $6,256.69 ½. The commissioners determined that the "costly" Habre de Venture improvements of 1794 were worth $1,588 more than the value of the improvements on the three Plenty package tracts at that time. Mildred Daniel was awarded Habre de Venture free and clear, and the children of Margaret received Plenty, which had been valued by the commissioners at $7,844.00 All parties accepted the findings of the equity court commission and approved its report August 20, 1827. [131]

When Mildred sold Habre de Venture in 1831, to her cousin, William Briscoe Stone, the sale ended nearly all the involvement of Thomas Stone's heirs in Charles County real estate.

---

131   Archives of Maryland, Maryland Hall of Records, Annapolis, MD., *Charles County Court Proceedings*, 1826-1829, pp. 272-286.

This photograph shows a c.1900 Habre de Venture as it appeared between about 1840 and 1930 during the occupancy of William Briscoe Stone, Margaret Graham Stone and Michael Robertson Stone. The segment of a circle configuration is barely discernible from this aspect.

Enoch Pratt Free Library

However, simply as a matter of related interest here, children of Margaret Stone Daniel continued a suit in the Charles County court that lasted from about 1795 through 1841. This was an effort to gain final settlement of the estates of Thomas Stone and his uncle Daniel of St. Thomas Jenifer. The suit was pursued by those who had inherited the responsibility of the executors of the estates of both Stone and Jenifer. It resulted apparently from the residual tangled affairs involving business relationships between Thomas and his uncle. They died three years apart, leaving much business unsettled between them.

By mid-1831 the greater Habre de Venture tract had been satisfactorily re-surveyed with ownership now clearly established for Mildred Stone Daniel. By indenture dated July 28, 1831 Mildred sold to her cousin, Gustavus Brown, for $2,823.00 the large western portion of Habre de Venture property which lay across Gambra and Hog Hole Runs, and a large section that joined the eastern boundary of the whole tract on the south. This package totaled 716 acres, nearly all of which had been added to Habre de Venture by Thomas Stone and was described in his patent of 1787. The boundaries of the new Gustavus Brown parcel were surveyed January 23, 1830 by Thomas Perry, Charles County surveyor. The Brown portion was identified in the Perry survey as the Third Part of Habre de Venture (Lot 3). [132]

On July 28, 1831 Mildred Stone Daniel visited the Charles County courthouse in Port Tobacco and there, for the record, formally relinquished her long-held claim to Habre de Venture. She sold the same day both the large Part 3 package to cousin Gustavus Brown, and the Part 1 (Lot 1) portion to cousin William Briscoe Stone, who at this time had called Habre de Venture home for several years.

It wasn't until 1848 that William B. Stone (son of Judge Michael Jenifer Stone) finally gained possession of the remaining portion of Lot 2 of Habre de Venture, which for many years was called Distrest Corrected. The 60 acres in this parcel were purchased May 1, 1848 from the heirs of Mildred who died in 1837. This transaction released the Stone-Daniels from the final bit

---

132 *C. C. Land Records, op.cit.* Liber JB19, pp. 391-395.

of real estate involvement in Charles County, over 60 years after the death of Thomas Stone. [133]

William Briscoe Stone died December 1, 1872. His very short and simple will, probated December 10, 1872, left half of his property, real and personal, to his unmarried daughter, Margaret Graham Stone. The other half was left to his wife, Caroline, to be used and held by her so long as she lived, and then the second half also was to go to daughter Margaret, now 47 years of age. W. B. Stone in his will says

> ... *I have excluded my two other children from this will and from any benefit under it not from any want of affection but from the fact that they have already received by way of advancement their full share of my property.*

His son, Thomas David, had long been comfortably situated on a valuable historic piece of agricultural land called Ellenborough near Pope's Creek. Throughout the years, W.B. Stone had contributed substantially to the economic condition of the Thomas D. Stone family. [134]

Port Tobacco lawyer and Maryland First Judicial District Judge W. B. Stone was in effect the "master" of Habre de Venture, particularly its improvements, for about 50 years, longer than anyone else. He seems to have been a thoroughly honest and faithful overseer for the ten or so years he managed Habre de Venture for his cousin Mildred. Even before he married, as early as 1821, his intimate involvement with the property was reflected in correspondence between him and first cousin Dr. John Moncure Daniel, Jr., of Falmouth, Virginia, son of Margaret Stone Daniel. [135]

---

133   *C. C. Land Records, op.cit.* Liber WM 3, pp. 75-77.

134   *C. C. Wills .op.cit.* William Briscoe Stone will probated December 10, 1872.

135   Duke University, Durham, NC, Special Collections, William Perkins Library, *William Briscoe Stone Collection.* Hereinafter, *W. B.Stone Collection.*

As mistress of Habre de Venture, Margaret Graham Stone lost little time in selling off a significant portion of her land, no doubt through great necessity. During Miss Margaret's tenure the farm had to support itself. There were very few outside sources of income. Law practice monies had kept Habre de Venture afloat for a century.

Late in the 19th century Frank Willing Leach, in his unpublished manuscript *Genealogy of the Signers of the Declaration of Independence*, could add nothing about the life of Thomas Stone not already known. His communication with Miss Margaret Graham Stone at Habre de Venture gave him no new information about the Signer, and Miss Margaret was a loyal Stone family historian who must have known as much about Thomas as any Thomas Stone descendant then living. [136]

Margaret, first born child of William Briscoe and Sarah Caroline Brown Stone, of the Rose Hill Browns, was born at Habre de Venture October 24, 1825. She died there February 22, 1913, having been mistress of the plantation from late 1872 until her death, a period of 40 years. She had desired to leave the entire estate to a cousin, Thomas Somervell Stone of Woodville/Acquasco, Prince George's County. His father was Dr. Michael Jenifer Stone, Jr. who practiced medicine in that area most of his adult life. Thomas S. had helped "Miss Margaret" run Habre de Venture. However, he showed no interest in inheriting this property; it is said he even destroyed the will which devised the

---

136   Frank Willing Leach, *Genealogy of the Signers of the Declaration of Independence*. Unpublished manuscript, c. 1886. Letter from Travers Daniel, Jr. whose grandmother was Margaret Stone Daniel: "Frederick Stone, only son died without issue. This Frederick Stone died . . . of yellow fever, contracted in Philadelphia where he had stopped in company with some fellow students on his return from Princeton College, New Jersey, and where he had taken his degree preparatory to entering the practice of law. He is recorded by his friend and fellow student, John Randolph of Roanoke, who was with him at the time of his death, as being a great genius and a prodigy in acquirement of his obituary written by Mr. Randolph - his noble character was greatly praised and his intellectual capacity and acquirement graphically described - This obituary was among the private papers of my grandmother, Margaret Stone."

estate to him. [137] Shortly before her death Margaret decided that Michael Robertson Stone, a son of her brother, Thomas David Stone of Ellenborough, would be a likely heir. He was left Habre de Venture by Margaret's will probated early in 1913. It appears that he and his family moved into the house sometime during 1913 after having lived at Ellenborough during the first three years of married life. [138]

As had all other male Stone owners of Habre de Venture M. R. Stone followed a full-time "outside" profession. He was a teacher and supervisor in the Charles County education system. He attempted, however, to make the Habre de Venture agricultural capacity support the property. But, as with the previous Stone proprietors it was always hard-going.

In 1931 Michael Robertson Stone died – the last of the Stones to possess Habre de Venture. He was the great grandson of Congressman and Judge Michael Jenifer Stone (1747-1812), a younger brother of Thomas. By deed dated January 21, 1936 the heirs of Michael Robertson Stone, represented by Richard Gough, trustee, sold Habre de Venture to Charles Stephenson Smith. Five of M. R. Stone and Bessie Gough Stone's seven children were born at Habre de Venture. The property conveyed to Mr. Smith was bounded exactly as it had been when it was willed to Michael Robertson Stone by his aunt in 1913.

On the 16th of January 1945, Charles Stephenson Smith sold Habre de Venture to Peter Vischer and Ruth Gardner Vischer. The deed called the total package Part of Habre de Venture and Part of Mattingly's Hope and was in accord with a survey made by Louis H. Steffens, Charles County surveyor, on November 19, 1935. [139]

Ruth Gardner Vischer died June 8, 1950 and her will left Habre de Venture to her husband. About a year later Peter Vischer married Helen C. Lombard. [140]

---

137   *Newman, op.cit.*

138   *C. C. Wills, op.cit.* Liber CHP 19, folio 512.

139   *C. C. Land Records, op.cit.* Liber TBM 81, folio 47.

140   *C. C. Wills, op.cit.* REC 23, pp. 357-366, probated Oct. 17, 1950.

While controlled by Peter and Helen C. Vischer the historic configuration of Habre de Venture property was changed notably by several transfers of ownership. Along the northern boundary the Vischers deeded a 5.8 acre package to John W. and Lillian Lorraine Thompson. The deed was dated August 19, 1952. The northern edge of this package followed the course of the abandoned Port Tobacco-Glymont road. [141] At the southern end of the property, over 17 acres were deeded by Helen Vischer to members of the Andrij and Nadija Lemko family. Details about Habre de Venture property changes 1682-1952 are documented in the 1988 National Park Service final report of the Stone family and Habre de Venture's history, written by the Wearmouths under contract with the National Park Service. [142]

Habre de Venture agricultural dependencies built about 1830-35 by William Briscoe Stone. L to r - tobacco barn, corn house, cattle barn. Photograph taken in 1986
John M. Wearmouth

---

141   *C. C. Land Records, op.cit.*, Liber 103, folio 23.

142   John M. Wearmouth, *Thomas Stone National Historic Site - Historic Resource Study. Part 1 - Biographical Sketch; Part 2 - Property History; Part 3 - Land Use History; Part 4 - Legislative History*, under Contract CX 4000-7-0029 with the National Park Service, May 11, 1988.

Habre de Venture Land Use

An understanding of the historic patterns and cycles of land use at Habre de Venture must be viewed in the light of changing southern Maryland society, economy and culture. One of the most penetrating, scholarly insights into Charles County, Maryland agricultural society in early colonial times is a work by Lorena Seebach Walsh entitled *Charles County, Maryland, 1658-1705: A Study of Chesapeake Political and Social Structure.* This was a doctoral thesis presented to the history department of Michigan State University in 1977. It provides a unique, thoroughly documented picture of life in this county at the time the Barefoots owned and farmed the original 150-acre Habre de Venture tract. [143]

This property comprised roughly the lower, southernmost one-third of the property purchased by Stone. The earliest years of formal agricultural production at Habre de Venture quite possibly reflected a frantic, ill-managed attempt to take advantage of the relatively high prices fetched by Maryland tobacco in the western European marketplaces near the end of the 17th century.

Small, upland plantations, such as Habre de Venture was initially, seldom were managed by those interested in wise, long-term soil husbandry.

In 1708 when John Barefoot sold his 150 acres to John Lambert (or Lambeth) the property included dwelling houses, barns, stables, gardens and outhouses, according to the deed dated May 24th of that year. All of this neatly fits the Walsh study description of small Charles County tobacco plantations during this period. The 500 pounds of tobacco Lambert paid Barefoot hardly reflects the transfer of ownership of a valuable piece of plantation property. In fact, the transaction quite likely indicates that the Barefoots simply had wrung out of the Habre de Venture acreage whatever they could in a short period of time while applying an absolute minimum of careful, educated husbandry to maintenance

---

143   Lorena Seebach Walsh, *Charles County, Maryland, 1658-1705: A Study of Chesapeake Political and Social Structure,* Ann Arbor, MI and High Wycombe, Bucks., England, 1977.

of the soil.

The 1783 Charles County Tax Assessment records furnish a sparse, interesting and "bare bones" picture of Habre de Venture's condition at this time. It still contained 442 acres, with half cleared. The land was described as

... *primarily poor and/or barren, or stiff.*

Less bleak was the description of the improvements – one good dwelling house, brick, a kitchen . . . other necessary houses. On the basis of this tax assessment it seems obvious that only about one half of Habre de Venture was productive agricultural land, hardly a sign of a prosperous, high-yield plantation. [144] The tax assessor's appraisal of Habre de Venture land conditions was supported about a century later when Thomas Stone's great grandson, Virginian Richard M. Conway, told Virginia genealogist Horace E. Hayden that Stone owned an unproductive farm – Habre de Venture – most of it

... *being quite thin land and needing cultivation.* [145]

In 1794 the Stone daughters divided up their brother's real estate inheritance in a way that seemed fair to both of them. Mildred chose Habre de Venture, primarily because it included extensive and valuable improvements, the one and one half story brick dwelling house in particular. She was aware that Habre de Venture lands were only marginally productive. Margaret chose the Plenty holdings just east of Port Tobacco Run and 1 ½ miles from Habre de Venture because of their extensive, highly productive lowland acres near the Run which for nearly a century and a half had been among the most desirable tobacco land in the county. [146]

The appearance of Habre de Venture as a marginally profitable farming establishment during Thomas Stone's stewardship indicates that he had little interest in agriculture as a

---

144   *C. C. Tax Assessment, op.cit.*

145,   *Hayden, op.cit.*

146   *C. C. Land Records, op.cit.*, Liber JB17, pp. 410-413.

source of income. Indeed, he spent relatively little time at this home between 1775 and the year he died. As a product of David Stone's second marriage, Thomas must always have known he probably would not, at least as a young man, be called upon to manage a plantation. And, simply by being members of this distinguished old family at Poynton Manor, Thomas and his brothers quite likely never were called upon to sweat or soil their hands in the fields.

Nowhere in Thomas Stone's letters is there even a mention of a manager or overseer at Habre de Venture. It seems odd that Stone's intense concern about the mill operation apparently did not extend to management of the Habre de Venture land. Quite possibly the farming effort at the plantation home was limited to a kind of subsistence agriculture that did not go beyond the production of staple foodstuffs, firewood, wool and construction supplies needed only to support the basic human needs of comfort, food and shelter. And, of course, both the field and household servants had to be provided for and there probably was at Habre de Venture between 1775 and 1787 a community numbering between 25 and 35 people, and a fair number of these were Stone family members born at Poynton Manor who for one reason or another sought shelter in the main dwelling at Habre de Venture – two of Thomas's sisters, a nephew and two brothers. Possibly his 1783 move to Annapolis was in part to escape the people congestion at the first home.

And, of course, both the field and household servants had to be provided for and there probably was at Habre de Venture between 1775 and 1787 a community numbering between 25 and 35 people, and a fair number of these were Stone family people born at Poynton Manor who for one reason or another sought shelter in the main dwelling at Habre de Venture – two of Thomas's sisters, a nephew and two brothers. Possibly his 1783 move to Annapolis was in part to escape the people congestion at the first home.

Until young lawyer William Briscoe Stone (1795-1872) began overseeing Habre de Venture about 1820 for his cousin Mildred Daniel the property saw few if any competent, devoted managers. Both Stone girls married and moved to Virginia by late

1793. Their uncle Michael Jenifer Stone married about 1794 and moved to his new home Equality a year ot two later. Probably he kept in touch with Habre de Venture until his death in 1812. Mildred's husband, Travers Daniel, Jr., was born and raised on a Virginia plantation, Crows Nest, where he lived until he died in 1823. Doubtless he made the major decisions about his wife's Charles County property for over a quarter of a century.

William B. Stone left his father's home, Equality, and married Sarah Caroline Brown of Rose Hill about 1823. They were living at Habre de Venture when their first child, Margaret Graham Stone, was born in 1825. Although this Stone practiced law as did Thomas, he seems to have taken farming more seriously than his distinguished uncle. Even before William came finally into possession of Habre de Venture about 1831, he prepared a lease agreement for consideration of his cousin Gustavus Brown of Rose Hill who was to become his new neighbor along the south end of the Stone land.

When the Signer purchased his acres in late 1770 from Daniel Jenifer he quite possibly found any dwelling house in only marginally useful condition. Stone's uncle Daniel Jenifer, brother of Daniel of St. Thomas, kept his property only about a year and a half after the newly formed holding was surveyed and found to contain 442 acres. Daniel Jenifer advertised in the *Maryland Gazette* that he planned to

> . . . *sell on April 3* [1769] *324 acres 1 ½ miles from town* [Port Tobacco] *part of Habre de Venture Enlarged and Hanson's Plains Enlarged. On this plantation are two tenements* [dwellings] *which rent for a crop hogshead each* [per year]. *The land is well watered and wooded, better for farming than planting.* [147]

This ad possibly was the first indication to Stone that his uncle's newly acquired property was for sale. This was a short item, but it reflects some interesting facts about the property soon after purchased by Stone. The advertisement indicates only 324 of the 442 acres were to be sold. The mention of tenements indicates

---

147   *Maryland Gazette,* Annapolis, Maryland, March 2, 1769.

the land under cultivation and perhaps being worked by two tenant farmers. The Jenifer comment about the land being

    ... better for farming than planting

may be reasonably interpreted as meaning the acres for sale were not considered desirable for tobacco production. One must assume that Stone knew from the very first walk around Habre de Venture the true "lay of the land." After all, he was born and raised a farmer's son about eight miles away. The property prospects simply provided all that Stone desired.

    At least one of the Stone daughters was born on Habre de Venture property – Mildred in 1770 according to the date on her tombstone in Stafford County, Virginia on the Daniel family Crows Nest plantation. The residence at Habre de Venture could not have been completed before early 1773. The Stones may have resided in one of the tenements found on the property when surveyed by Hanson in 1768.

    The Thomas Stone family left Habre de Venture to take up their much more sophisticated town life in Annapolis about mid-1783, leaving the estate in the hands of family members living there who no doubt were more interested in the roof over their heads than the productivity of the surrounding fields. About a year later Stone began to reduce his Habre de Venture agricultural inventory through sales at Port Tobacco. In November 1784 he sold at his Great Port Tobacco Mill on Port Tobacco Run (about ½ mile up-stream from the village), slaves, horses, sheep, cattle and plantation utensils. Certainly from this point on Habre de Venture's value as a commercially desirable plantation must have been sharply reduced.

    The Library of Congress's *Stone Family Collection of Maryland* includes many bits of business correspondence between Thomas Stone and his brother Walter at Port Tobacco and between brother John Hoskins Stone and Walter who managed John's tobacco business in Charles County. [148]

    Thomas Stone's primary concern about farm production had to do with livestock, including hogs, corn and wheat. Perhaps the condition of Habre de Venture's land, combined with the labor-intensive nature of tobacco production, turned Stone away from

---

148   LC - *Stone Family of Maryland, op.cit.*

this crop. His successful law practice during the last fifteen years of his life certainly more than compensated for benefits that may have been realized from major emphasis on tobacco production.

During the last three years of his life Thomas Stone seems to have been increasingly concerned about money matters. There was a shortage of specie throughout Maryland. The Treaty of Paris had brought peace but not prosperity, as broadly anticipated. Tobacco planters were disappointed and distressed beyond measure over low tobacco prices. Letters from both John Hoskins and Thomas to Walter indicate a great depth of concern over the state of the economy and their own solvency.

RES. OF THO⁵. STONE
Port Tobacco Mᵈ

In a March 11, 1785 letter to Walter at Port Tobacco, Thomas asks his brother to help get court writs against people who owe him money. In a letter dated April 22, Thomas asks Walter to handle many business affairs for him in Charles County and to collect as much as possible for debts owed him. Walter is asked even to account for crops sold or to be sold, which are produced on Stone family plantations. Thomas now is concerned about how best to use the slaves he has left in the county and discusses where they are employed, who has been hired out and who should be or will be. He lists his livestock and mentions a "trifle" of furniture left at Habre de Venture, plus two carts and two oxen. He asks if his debtors in Charles County have left money for him with Walter, saying

> am in want of anything due me, I must have it.

He describes his ill health and says

> as fast as I move a step forward I am drawn as
> much back by a repetition by the disorder.

Then, late in the fall, a similar letter from Thomas on November 24 asks Walter what notes he has for him as

> I want to sue everybody who owes me and will not
> pay . . . I want much to have all my affairs settled –
> I shall have some negroes to hire next year,
> including carpenter Tom with his tools . . . as well
> as Bob . . . also a couple of the women with their
> children for anything above victuals and clothes . . .

Thomas is now worried about how to employ the slaves he has left in Charles County, reflecting a lessened requirement for them at Habre de Venture. A slave named Gus would be offered for hire for three pounds a year. Then, in the same letter Stone asks for Walter's help in hiring out Negroes for the following year, including some skilled craftsmen. [149]

Another indication of Stone's decreasing involvement in Habre de Venture farming is documented in the April 22 letter to Walter. In another measure of Habre de Venture's reduced farming operations, Thomas asks Walter to have his Port Tobacco miller, Thomas Ostro, send 40 bushels of corn to Habre de Venture and

---

149   *Ibid.*

complains that the miller has not yet sent the amount of wheat due him. By early 1787 the relatively small, 20-acre mill establishment on Port Tobacco Run seems to have become Stone's major farming establishment. These 20 acres included the mill and were used for raising hogs and certain crops, probably including corn and wheat.[150]

Thomas must always have known he probably would not, at least as a young man, be called upon to manage the Poynton Manor plantation. And, simply by being members of this distinguished old family at its large estate, Thomas and his brothers quite likely never were called upon to sweat or soil their hands in the fields. For the most part none of them ever did. David Stone owned between 50 and 60 slaves – more than enough labor supply for Poynton Manor. Nowhere in Thomas Stone's letters is there even a mention of a manager or overseer at Habre de Venture. It seems odd that Stone's intense concern about the mill operation apparently did not extend to management of the Habre de Venture land. Quite possibly the farming effort at the plantation home was limited to a kind of subsistence agriculture that did not go beyond the production of staple foodstuffs, firewood, wool and construction supplies.

150   *Ibid.*

The Stone Jewel

Habre de Venture's main dwelling house completed about 1773 by Thomas Stone was ever the dignified and striking centerpiece of the Stone domain. During the 20th Century several architects and writers waxed mellow and enthused about the "mansion's" unique design, construction and orientation on its site. All commented upon the full house complex being constructed in a segment of a circle. Whether Stone himself ever set eyes on the old house as it appeared in late 20th Century may fairly be doubted. In our opinion only the principal central mass may without much doubt reflect the product of 1771-73 as Thomas and Margaret knew it.

A wood engraving print done about 1830 shows in clear line-form what the west elevation (terrace side) looked like then. This print shows no house-linked structure at the south end leading to the "law office" appendage long in place. Leading off the north end appears the one-story brick hyphen leading nowhere. This hyphen is made of very old excellent Flemish bond brickwork that in no way matches that in the central mass walls. This oddly dimensioned, shallow-pitch roof structure is built of brick similar to possibly late 17th Century brickwork fronting the sacristy of St. Ignatius Roman Catholic church about six miles away at Chapel Point. In fact, Habre de Venture displays three styles of brick work in its walls, including that in the c.1840 kitchen unit.

The two house-length piazzas (porches) probably were of initial design and construction – welcome respite from the often scorching southern Maryland summers: The only air conditioning known. Habre de Venture really is a three story affair with a full basement and enough window-light to offset the dungeon-like atmosphere of below-grade living areas. Quite possibly the house-help lived here in more than usual comfort of field hands.

In any event, William Briscoe Stone, living here as a tenant of his cousin Mildred Stone Daniel, sent her a detailed breakdown of repairs he had supervised at Habre de Venture during 1825. It seems no major repairs were done on

main building – I have had the top of the roof . . .
covered – it took about 12,000 shingles.

155

1928 E. H. Pickering photograph of the west facade, which overlooked a terraced yard and long, raised walkway.   Baltimore Museum of Art

This legal-size three page letter includes breakdowns of supplies and services paid for during the year.

In addition to minor "main house" repairs W. B. S. planned and oversaw the building of a new stable, corn house and wash house. The amounts and types of supplies purchased by him more than hint at construction of a new, good size building – orders for brass knobs and locks, panes, bricks, putty and joiner work all point to a rather large, sophisticated structure apart from the peripheral dependencies. Quite likely we see here the considerable effort made by Stone to rebuild a destroyed kitchen. We do know that about 1810 a violent (likely a tornado) storm smashed down two large masonry structures in Port Tobacco one and a half miles away. Or, as so often happened with country kitchens . . . a fire possibly took it. We still do not know how Thomas Stone's kitchen looked.

Sometime prior to 1840 Stone sent a cold and unfriendly note to Port Tobacco merchant John Fergusson, living at Mulberry Grove. Apparently Fergusson had not furnished promised skilled carpenter help (probably slave) to Habre de Venture for a new kitchen complex. W. B. S. weeps a bit as he says

> . . . *I have suffered so much in my little family*
> *comforts concerning for want of our kitchen – &*
> *the time notably elapsed when you promised to send*
> *your man that I could wait patiently at last no*
> *longer.*

Finally, Stone reminds Fergusson about his tutoring of Fergusson boys at Habre de Venture – in effect meeting all promises in this respect. This letter is undated, but probably followed the letter to Mildred by several years.

On January 16, 1826 a memorandum about exchange of carpenter slave laborers was drawn up in a neat hand by Mrs. Gustavus Brown at Rose Hill, the property touching Habre de Venture along its southern boundary

> . . . *Stone's man Harry and Mrs. Brown's Sam to*
> *work for W . B. S. as carpenters on the 13th of*
> *March and Mr. Stone's man Harry and Mrs.*
> *Brown's man Sam went to Mrs. Brown's to "set*
> *up."*

On the 19th of March Lewis and Anthony went to Mr. Stone's.
Lewis and Anthony returned to Mrs. Brown May 25th and Sam on
the 4th of June, Harry on the 7th of June. Mrs. Brown wrote

> *. . . I discharged Harry on the 15th of August and*
> *Sam on 22nd August 1826.*

So, from March 13 to the middle of August 1826 some rather
major construction projects were underway at Habre de Venture
and Rose Hill. [151]

On March 8, 1830 and again on March 17, 1835,
Alexandria merchant Thomas Swann shipped fifteen barrels of
plaster to Port Tobacco for W. B. Stone. He informs the master of
Habre de Venture that

> *Capt. Brookbank will deliver you the plaster*
> *according to order and the freight which is 12/2 per*
> *barrel.*

The bill for the plaster was written at the bottom of this letter at a
total cost of $22.50. [152] This period squares nicely with the usual
conjectural age of the new kitchen wing attached to the ancient
north hyphen. The 1835 shipment dovetails with the approximate
date of Stone's letter to his two daughters at school telling them
about the still wet plastered walls – in a structure not specified, but
it appeared that the newly finished walls would be of prime
importance to the girls. In 1835, daughter Margaret was ten years
old and sister Mary about eight. Incidentally, the cost of the trans-
Potomac plaster delivery almost equaled the purchase price of the
merchandise. [153]

A W. B. Stone letter (by Charley) to daughters Margaret
and Mary suggest several years were needed to complete the added
north wing. No doubt the kitchen facilities in the structure were
finished as soon as possible – on the ground floor. The second
floor rooms may well not have been finished until about 1840 as

---

151   *W. B. Stone Collection, op.cit,* Memorandum recording laborers
(carpenters) from Mrs. Gustavus Brown to William B. Stone, January 16, 1826.

152   *MHS 406, op.cit.*

153   *Ibid.* Letters March 8, 1830 and March 17, 1835 from Thomas Swann of
Alexandria, Virginia to William B. Stone, Esq.

Habre de Venture, c. 1936. The dining room in the hyphen connecting main house to the kitchen wing on the northwest side of "crescent" complex.

Stone told his girls (in school at Forest Hall Institute, St. Mary's County)

> *. . . the neglect of workmen – the delay because of rain – our old house is yet unfinished – the plastering is much too wet for use – we must bear perforce for some tome to come this inconvenience.* [154]

At this time the daughters Margaret and Mary, both on the threshold to adulthood, certainly forced the Stones into providing added bedroom space – quite likely the finishing of two large bedrooms above the kitchen. These rooms were finely finished and trimmed out in the then popular late Federal Period fashion. At this time Stone son Thomas David and 20-year orphaned cousin Frederick probably lived at Habre de Venture studying law under William's tutorship. So, the increased inventory of bedrooms reflected a growing need as the younger generation developed. Incidentally, both W. B. and nephew Frederick became members of Maryland's Court of Appeals. These Stones descended from Thomas's younger brother, Michael Jenifer Stone, local judge and member of the First Congress of the United States, 1789-91.

The charming south-flank frame structure at Habre de Venture has been accepted for years as being contemporary with the central mass and the location of Thomas Stone's law office. This 16 ½ by 18 ½ foot building is connected to the house by an ancient breeze way leading to a large and very attractive basement entrance door quite possibly of 18th Century construction. The building is one story and a half with a two-pitch Maryland style gambrel roof – post and beam construction and sheathed with clapboard siding. The brick chimney in the southeast wall displays mortar made with Portland cement – a revealing age factor. Two circular-sawn summer beams rest on cemented brick piers. Tongue and groove floor planks are fastened to partially hand-hewn joints by machine cut and wire nails. These facts lead one to doubt the "law office" was ever such in the 18th Century. In 1986, under contract with the National Park Service, Ron Deiss undertook an

---

154   *Ibid.*

archeological investigation of the "law office" site before serious restoration took place. [155]   In April 1986 three volunteer archeologists began to survey ground around the "office." A major finding was that the structure and the foundation under it did not square. There was a firm suggestion that the "law office" was moved from another site – quite possibly just before mid-19th Century. The use of Portland cement indicates a c.1840-1850 construction (or reconstruction) time. Findings pointed to an earlier structure on the same site because the uncovered foundation once supported a structure of different dimensions. Close examination of the soil beneath the floor may have disclosed evidence of a fire – one that may have destroyed an earlier kitchen under the stewardship of W. B. Stone. If so, when a new kitchen complex appeared at the north end, connected by a hyphen of considerable age, the "law office" site may have been used to serve a new purpose. Stone mentions in his 1825 letter to Mildred Daniel his working to repair or enhance a washhouse. [156] The semi-open covered hyphen leading from the" law office" to the basement would have offered kitchen workers an all-season, convenient way to deliver prepared food to the 18th Century Stone residents. Possibly a dumb waiter lifted meals up and into the dining room.

In 1985 university students from several major U.S. colleges of architecture worked for the Historic American Building Survey (HABS) during the summer to analyze the entire Habre de Venture complex and produce professional-grade architectural drawings now part of the HABS records.

The main dwelling structure of Habre de Venture needs nothing beyond its modest, dignified setting to mark it as one of the charming survivors of the Middle Atlantic States' Colonial Period architectural treasures. It is not large by house standards of then or now. True, its four great rooms and broad up and down center hallway, front to back, provide much square footage of space but

---

155   Ron Deiss, *Archaeological Excavations at the Thomas Stone Historic Site,* for National Park Service, 1986, Port Tobacco, Maryland.

156   *MHS 406, op.cit.* Letter from William B. Stone to Mildred Stone Daniel written late in 1825.

with sacrifice of privacy and entertainment facilities. Doubtless the years of the Stones' greatest comfort in their new home preceded the onslaught of other family members in desperate need of permanent shelter.

Maryland architect James Thomas Wollon, Jr., A.I.A. as a prerequisite major step toward plans for reconstruction after the tragic fire in 1977, presented his Habre de Venture Historic Structure Report to the National Park Service in July 1987. Architect Wollon correctly asserts that the main house, as flanked by its hyphen-connected satellite structures, produces

> . . . *one of the more picturesque houses of its period.*

Probably the most exquisite feature of the house was the floor-to-ceiling parlor panel work sold by the Michael R. Stone to the Baltimore Museum of Art in 1928, said to have come from the parlor. Sale of this paneling no doubt was the 20th century's most significant house change aside from the fire damage of 1977. It led to a new second floor for the west hyphen to make room for a modern bathroom facility. Part of the deal in the museum's acquisition was that the package include Robert Edge Pine's mid-1785 oil portrait of Thomas – perhaps today valued high above the dollar value of all the paneling.

The National Park Service architect's report on the central mass describes the excellent brickwork well. As he states in the report, the very intense heat of the 1977 fire did little damage to the exterior walls that display a most pleasing Flemish bond aspect below the eaves. Brickwork above this level, including upper parts of the large, double flue end chimneys, is laid in English bond. It is often said, "Out of sight often out of Flemish." It was always the most expensive type of brick construction. An interesting brick laying treatment may be seen where a few courses of English bond in the brick chimney gable ends soften the transition from Flemish to common bond.

The design and placement of the exquisite transom lights above both principal doorways presented a well lighted main central hallway on the first floor level even on a dull day of winter. The north side transom was situated to brighten the large landing that broke the two flights leading upstairs. These transoms measured

Parlor paneling at Habre de Venture before its move to Baltimore Museum of Art c.1927. Photograph by E. H. Pickering.

Baltimore Museum of Art

about 46" x 35" and included 15 panes each.

The architect describes the very old central mass exterior wall brick inscriptions well and was properly concerned about preservation of the inscribed bricks. The great piazza roofs protected them for years. Both Stone and Brown family members (children and adults) left their marks in the Habre de Venture walls. These inscriptions are neatly and artfully done – indicating it was quite acceptable to the home owners. The David Stone inscriptions (likely Thomas's father) low in south wall bricks are sharp and clean – one says "AUG. 1772." Somehow the names and initials link us more closely with Habre de Venture figures of yesteryear.

A very old friend of Habre de Venture in an interview taped about 1985 remembered the tiny upper hall room (sometimes referred to as the "trunk room") of the south side. It was used by Margaret Stone's dwarfish black girl, Mariah, who was Miss Margaret's sole companion and helpmate about 1895-1910 in the old mansion. [157]

The architect concludes that the central Habre de Venture block was

typical of the period and region . . . for a dwelling of this class.

Possibly so . . . but those who designed, constructed, lived at and were born in the old "manse" gave it a quality of being attained first during its 18th century years when Thomas, Margaret, son Frederick and daughters Mildred and Margaret gave life and warmth to both outside and inside walls. The family had its share of suffering. Once Thomas could not get to Annapolis sessions of the Maryland Convention because those at home had contracted a very contagious, often deadly disease. Thomas himself released house servants and nursed his family back to survivable conditions. Daughter Margaret, still at Habre de Venture in late 1793, was devastated by news of her brother's death of yellow fever at Princeton about September 4.

---

157 Taped interview by John M. Wearmouth with Lorena Butler Chambers in 1985 about Mariah; describes dining with Mariah and Miss Stone in old hyphen kitchen, c.1908.

1928 E. H. Pickering photograph of the east facade which faced the road only about 100 feet away. Piazza here covered a brick paved floor.   Baltimore Museum of Art

On December 15, 1793 Margaret experienced happier times when she married Dr. John Moncure Daniel of Falmouth, Virginia. This affair took place at the great house and perhaps included the greatest assemblage of aristocratic, distinguished persons ever sheltered at one time under the splendid gambrel roof. Margaret's uncle, Michael Jenifer Stone, most likely gave her away. He had served his two-year term in the First Congress of the United States and after his brother's death was guardian of the three Stone children. Sister Mildred doubtless attended this wedding with her Virginia husband, Travers Daniel, Jr. of Stafford County. He was the brother of the groom. And, of course, all the Doctor Gustavus Richard Brown clan from Rose Hill and elsewhere would have been present.

It may be said fairly that at least the Habre de Venture main structure tells us even now quite a lot about the family that designed and built this charming and distinguished country house. Both Margaret and Thomas were from and were nurtured by sophisticated aristocratic life styles. They were welcome in Charles County's finest homes – those owned by the creme de la creme of southern Maryland's plantation society. Margaret's father, the venerable Dr. Gustavus Brown, had been a renowned successful physician here for about half a century. But, Thomas's distinguished family was not wealthy. The mansion house of Habre de Venture reflects the good taste, sophistication and refined humility of a couple unspoiled by family position of long standing. The old central mass reflects a beautiful, enduring display of the qualities of mind, heart and soul of its first owners. They rest side by side in a tiny family burial plot only about 400 feet from their gracious old house. In spite of similarities to local contemporaneous architecture Habre de Venture remains unique with its own remarkable personality.

Because of research, including archeology, in the late 20th Century, one may question whether Margaret and Thomas ever saw the old house as it long stood in regal dignity anchoring today's two adjoining wings. As previously stated, an 1825-35 sketch of the south (terrace) side shows nothing of the south "office" wing, and the brick hyphen at the north end seems attached to nothing. Between about 1825 and 1840 William B. Stone struggled to complete the new multi-purpose north "kitchen" wing. We cannot be sure where the original kitchen stood, although archeology has left some clues.

Nearly 100 years after Thomas Stone's death the following details of a reporter's visit to his Port Tobacco home appeared in the *Maryland Independent*, a Charles County newspaper.

An Interesting Sketch of a Visit to Our County
Below we publish extracts from a letter written to the <u>New York Tribune</u> by a recent visitor to our County that may prove interesting to some of our readers.

> *During the past week I made a visit to some of the old slave counties of Maryland on the lower Potomac River and enjoyed riding through as picturesque a country as can be found anywhere on our navigable tidal waters. The hills are very high above the bottoms and streams and are beautifully wooded with oaks and chestnuts and occasional pine forests, the latter which is taken off the malaria which still is the curse of much of this country.*

> *. . . I paid a visit to the grave of a signer of the Declaration of Independence last week and was delighted to find how perfectly his home and property are retained in his family. There were but four signers of the Declaration from Maryland, the youngest of whom was Thomas Stone. He lived about two miles from Port Tobacco on an estate called Havredeventure. His house, which was finished about 1771, is made of brick with one high story with a second story in the broken gable, and there are wings retiring from the building on a segment of a circle, in one which was his office. One of the large rooms in the main building is wainscoted to the roof [ceiling] and contains his portrait painted by Pine [Robert Edge]. His next neighbor was the celebrated [Dr.] Gustavus [Richard] Brown, who was called in to attend the last illness of General Washington. The Stone*

Parlor paneling of c.1772 as installed at the Baltimore Museum of Art in 1964. Room furnishings are proper for the period, not of the Stone family. The portrait on right is of Margaret Stone's mother, Mrs. Gustavus Brown of Rich Hill.

*estate, in nearly its original proportions, is now
managed by a maiden lady, Miss Margaret
[Graham] Stone, who takes great pride in the family
matters and showed me some elegant antique
furniture and the measuring glass and medicine
chest of Dr. Brown. Passing through an oat field
on the flank of the house I came upon a clump of
cedars where lay the signer and his wife who died
but a few months apart, and her death broke his
heart at the early age of forty-four. The inscription*
[on the grave stone] *is as follows: Thomas Stone,
son of David and Elizabeth Stone, departed this life
October 5, 1787, age forty-four years. The
Archives of Maryland will show the offices of trust
he has held. He was an able and faithful lawyer, a
wise and virtuous patriot, an honest and good man.
The signer's brother, Michael Jenifer Stone, was
chief justice of the State and grandfather of the
present judge* [Honorable Frederick Stone], *who
studied law in this old house under William B.
Stone, his uncle* [and father of Margaret G. Stone,
owner in 1883 of Habre de Venture].

 *While I am on antiquities I may say I also
visited the grave of Washington's physician, Dr.
Brown. He had one of the very large mansions
overlooking the River Potomac built about 1760
with an elegant garden falling in terraces from its
front. There were no medical colleges in the land at
that time and he took medical students and they
dissected bodies under* [in the basement]. [158]

---

158 *Maryland Independent,* Port Tobacco, MD, Friday, June 22, 1883.

As a National Park Service Historic Site

Soon after the disastrous fire on New Year's Day, 1977, destroyed the interior of the main central structure and the roof of Habre de Venture, Charles County and the State of Maryland moved quickly to acquire and restore what was left. On October 31, 1977, Maryland Senator Charles McC. Mathias, Jr. convened a meeting with State and local historical groups to discuss the future of Habre de Venture, then one of a few remaining original homes of Signers of the Declaration of Independence. This meeting led to negotiations between the Maryland Historical Trust and those who owned Habre de Venture. The purpose was to preserve and rebuild the Thomas Stone home near Port Tobacco in Charles County, Maryland, only a 45-minute drive from the Nation's Capital.

In great part because of local and State of Maryland interest, the United States Secretary of the Interior was directed by Congress late in 1978 to acquire

> ... by donation, exchange, or purchase with
> donated or appropriated funds, the Thomas Stone
> home and grounds, known as Habre-de-Venture,
> located on Rose Hill Road near La Plata in Charles
> County, Maryland, for establishment as the Thomas
> Stone National Historic Site. [159]

Specifically, acquisition of Habre de Venture was Federally mandated by Sec. 510. (A) Thomas Stone National Historic Site of Subtitle A – Parks, Seashores, etc. of TITLE V- Establishment of New Areas and Additions to National Trails System. This pertinent Section was included in the Legislative History of the National Parks and Recreation Act of 1978 (Public Law 95-625), known as "The Omnibus Act." The new Section 510. (A) under TITLE V was approved November 10, 1978. It allowed the National Park Service, United States Department of the Interior, to use up to (but not to exceed) $600,000 of appropriated Federal Government funds to acquire the Habre de Venture property and any interests in it, and not to exceed $400,000 for development.

---

[159] *Congressional Record,* July 10, 1978 and October 12, 1978.

Habre de Venture as restored by National Park Service as of the year 2000. East side above – west side below at the Thomas Stone National Historic Site.

Photos John M. Wearmouth

Government officials hoped that the site could be restored to its full beauty and operated as a working colonial residence and farm, much like the National Park Service had done at the birthplace of George Washington. On October 12, 1978, Senator Charles McC. Mathias, Jr., from Maryland, commented in the Senate

> . . . *on behalf of Senators Sarbanes, Humphrey, and Case, I am pleased to see that the subcommittee* [on National Parks and Insular Affairs] *has included in this bill* [P.L. 95-625] *the Thomas Stone house, known as Habre de Venture, as a national historic site and has authorized its acquisition . . . this* . . . *bill will permit the acquisition, restoration, refurbishing, and opening to the public of this grand Georgian mansion . . . The property has the potential of becoming a unique cooperative effort between private historic preservation groups and the National Park Service, perhaps ultimately as a working colonial farm.* [160]

On January 8, 1981, the U. S. Department of the Interior purchased the Habre de Venture property from Charles Lombard, trustee for Helen C. Vischer. The federal government paid $524,700.00 for 321.9 acres, all that remained of the package of 442 acres purchased in 1770 by Thomas Stone. Still, Habre de Venture boundaries of the late 20th century run amazingly near those of the 1768 patent awarded Daniel Jenifer. [161]

On October 9, 1988 the newest National Historic Site was introduced to primarily local people. This open house display was in effect a progress report and guests could see that much was yet to be done toward significant restoration of the main house and peripheral out-buildings. At this event the National Park Service was able to show the public the architect's drawings. And the two year effort of the authors was reflected in the final 1988 report to the National Park Services Region III Office in Philadelphia. This

---

160   *Ibid.*

161   *C. C. Land Records, op.cit.,* Liber 759, folio 81.

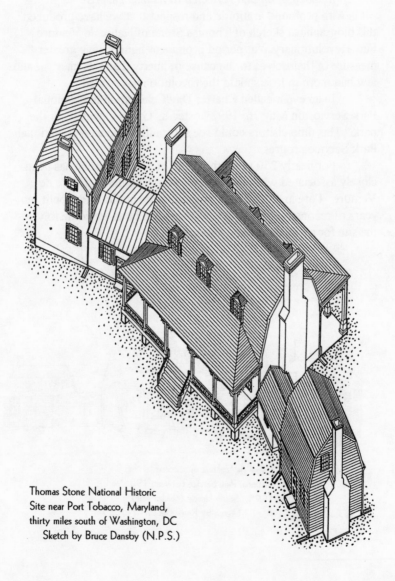

Thomas Stone National Historic
Site near Port Tobacco, Maryland,
thirty miles south of Washington, DC
Sketch by Bruce Dansby (N.P.S.)

detailed work included drawings of Habre de Venture property surveys from late 17th Century through about 1950. In the printed program for this event appeared a few very meaningful words

. . . the spirit and directions of the Nation are
founded upon and reflected in its historic past.

It is with profound gratitude and respect that we have produced this biographical sketch of Thomas Stone of Habre de Venture. Few Revolutionary War period prominent figures gave greater measure of themselves to the cause of liberty than this man . . . and few had more to lose should the revolution have failed.

In an event called Charter Day Celebration the National Park Service on May 16, 1992 hosted a "Grand Opening" at the park. This time visitors could see substantial evidence of National Park Service progress.

For nearly 250 years the name of Thomas Stone has been closely associated with his southern Maryland home, Habre de Venture. Late in 1998 it was opened to the public after about ten years of reconstruction effort. Visitors had been welcome to visit the site for a decade – since about 1988.

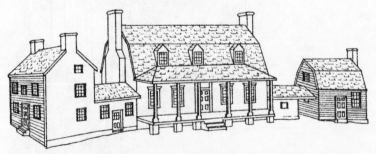

Habre de Venture as restored by the
National Park Service between 1985 and
1995. South facade (garden side).
Sketch by Bruce Dansby (N.P.S.)

Part V
Public Career

Following is the impressive record of Stone's public offices at local, State and Federal levels of government. How could anyone ask more of one patriot trying desperately to perform well in public service, provide for a young family miles from Annapolis and Philadelphia, while at the same time managing a new, thriving law practice?

Legislative Service
Local:

As part of an almost universal Colonial response to the Stamp Act, Charles County, Maryland played an active part in forcing repeal of this totally obnoxious Crown legislation. On June 14, 1774 at the Courthouse in Port Tobacco, prominent county men joined to protest the British blockade of Boston harbor following the Boston Tea Party.

Then, at Colony level in Annapolis, Thomas Stone and eighteen other county men voiced Maryland's abhorrence at closing Boston harbor. Stone served with about 100 other county men in the local Committee of Correspondence. At a meeting in Port Tobacco on November 18, 1774 Thomas Stone was designated a member of the "executive" group of ten authorized to speak for the entire 100-man Committee of Correspondence. This smaller group (ultimately thirteen members) was given authority to represent their County in Annapolis at the Provincial Convention, and speak for it in matters considered by the Maryland Convention. The Convention voted in 1775 to send Charles County's Thomas Stone to represent the State in the proceedings of the Second Continental Congress.

State Conventions representing Charles County

1st, 1774, 2nd-3rd, 1774; 4th, 1775; 5th, 1775; 6th - 8th, 1775-1776 (did not attend the 7th Convention).
Senate, Western Shore, Term of 1776-1781; 1777, 1777-1778, 1778-1779, 1780-1781 (resigned on December 19, 1780; re-elected and qualified on December 23, 1780).

the 1780-1781 Assembly to fill vacancy; resigned on December 26, 1780).
Senate, Western Shore, Term of 1781-1786, 1781-1782, 1782-1783, 1783 (did not attend), 1784, 1785, Term of 1786-1791, 1786-1787, 1787 (died before the 1st session of 1787-1788 Assembly).

Other State Office
1st Council of Safety, Western Shore, 1776 (elected, but did not serve).

Local Offices
Elected visitor of St. John's College, Annapolis, February 28, 1786.
Recorder, Annapolis, appointed October 1786, resigned by October 1787.

Social Status
Member of the Forensic Club in Annapolis, c. 1763-1766.

Out of State Service
Delegate, Continental Congress, 1774 (elected in December 1774, but no meetings of Congress were held), 1775-1776 (elected in April 1775, August 1775, May 1776, July 1776 and November 1776; no evidence of attendance after October 1776), 1777 (elected in February 1777, but did not attend; declined to serve on February 22, 1777), 1777-1778 (elected in December 1777, but did not attend until September 1778), 1783-1784 (elected in November 1783 but did not attend until March 1784).
Delegate Federal Convention that formed the Constitution 1787 (elected but declined to serve). [162]

Calendar of Maryland State Papers
        In 1941 the State of Maryland Hall of Records launched an incredibly demanding, long-term work to calendar the State's extraordinary, ancient collections of governmental records in its

---

[162] *MHR Biographical Dictionary, op.cit.*

This dignified "full Stone" portrait has hung in the old Maryland Senate Chamber since painted by John Beale Bordley about 1838. It was commissioned by the Assembly, most appropriately.   Maryland State Archives

custody – spanning over three centuries. First released in the Calendar series was the 1948 *Brown Books* by Roger Thomas. [163]

In late 1950 the Hall of Records released the first part of the *Rainbow Series* within the Hall of Records. There were (based on color of the hard cover) black, blue and brown books, all in print before the incredible red books went to the printer

> . . . *the last and by far the largest and most*
> *important of the State record groups.*

The State Archivist, Morris L. Radoff, anticipated in 1950 that two more "rainbow books" must be produced to calendar the State's entire collection. Part 1 of the two-volume *Red Book* set required eighteen months to complete. In it were 1,444 documents numbered, abstracted and indexed to furnish a streamlined and concise calendar of great value to all students of Maryland's past. For nearly half a century researchers have found the *Rainbow Series* to be priceless finding mediums.

The *Red Book* indices aid the researcher directly to the numbered abstracts. In this we can see that the July 27, 1775 vote of the Convention of Maryland shows clearly how and where Thomas Stone positioned himself with respect to a newly formed Committee

> *to put the Province in a state of defense.*

The Convention vote for Committee members shows that Stone received 16 votes – the same as Matthew Tilghman, Thomas Johnson, Samuel Chase, Robert Goldsborough and William Paca. This new Committee directed all of Maryland's effort to create armed forces that could and would challenge the King's will by force of arms – all this a year before the Declaration of Independence. And Stone was obviously thought by the Convention to be rebel enough to be activated to help a very distinguished and able group of Maryland's finest and most bellicose members of the Convention.

---

163 Roger Thomas, *Brown Books - No. 3, Calendar of Maryland State Papers,* Annapolis, MD., 1948.

The *Red Book* indices disclose in many entries the nature
and scope of Stone labors on behalf of his State and the evolving
new United States of America. [164]

Calendar of Maryland State Papers
Number 4, Part 1
The Red Books

(3 II, 80) Apr. 24-May 3, 1775 - Convention of Maryland.
"Short Notes of the Proceedings of April Convention 1775";
members attending Charles County: Capt. Francis Ware, Josias Hawkins, John
Dent, Thomas Stone, Daniel Jenifer, Robert T[ownsend] Hooe. Matthew
Tilghman, chairman; Gabriel Duvall, clerk; resolutions adopted to keep door
shut while in session, to allot 80 stand of arms for Annapolis, to allot two-
thirds of the remaining arms to the Western Shore and one-third to the Eastern
Shore, to insert the names of the members absent on May 1 in the *Maryland
Gazette*; committee appointed "to revise the proceedings for the press."

(17 II, 2) July 26-Aug. 14, 1775 - Convention of Maryland. "Short Notes" of
the proceedings: members present listed by counties: Charles: Daniel Jenifer,
Robert Townsend Hooe, William Harrison, John H[oskins] Stone, Samuel
Hanson, Jr., William Smallwood, Thomas Stone, John Dent, Philip Richard
Fendall. Printed in *Archives of Maryland.*, XI, 3-15

(18 II, 28) July 27, 1775, [Convention of Maryland]
Talley of votes for members of Committee "to put the Province in a
State of Defence" as follows: . . . . . . Tilghman 16, Johnson 16, Chase 16,
Goldsborough 16, Stone 16, Paca 16, Carroll of Carrollton 11, Johnson 1,
Carroll, Barrister 13, Holliday 11, Hall 5, Tilghman 3, Smyth 1, Brooke 1,
Lloyd 2. Endorsed "Ballot paper No. 1"

(22 II, 24) Aug. 2, 1775 - Convention of Maryland. Tally of votes for members
of committee "to shut up Courts of Justice; votes cast for . . . T[homas] S[tone],
. . .

(25 II, 3, 4, 6) - Aug. 14, 1775 - Convention of Maryland. Resolutions adopted
prescribing the "Association" to be signed by "freemen" of the province;
providing for the enrollment of minute-men and militia; establishing the
council of safety; providing for the printing of bills of credit; appointing

---

164 *Red Books – Parts I and II, Calendar of Maryland State Papers,* Hall
of Records Commission No. 7, (Annapolis, MD., 1950.)

treasurer for the Western Shore and treasurer for the Eastern Shore; providing for the election of committees of observation for each county; encouraging erection of saltpeter works and powder mill; requiring committees of observation to appoint persons to receive contributions of money and account for same; requiring committees of observation to account for all arms purchased in their county; naming Council of Safety members of Eastern and Western Shore - Thomas Stone appointed for Western Shore; ordering colonels to deliver arms to such captains of minute-men as the Council of Safety shall direct; naming deputies to the Continental Congress - Thomas Stone one of appointed, along with Matthew Tilghman, Thomas Johnson, Jr., Robert Goldsborough, William Paca, Samuel Chase and John Hall; setting third Tuesday of March 1776 as date of next meeting of Convention. Printed in *Archives of Maryland*, XI, 9-10, 15-31, 33-35 and in *Convention Proceedings*, 19-33, 35-36.

(33 II, 26) Aug, 14?, 1775 - Convention of Maryland. Tally of votes for "Continental Deputies"; Matthew Tilghman, Thomas Johnson, Samuel Chase, John Hall, Robert Goldsborough, Thomas Stone, William Paca elected; other nominees: Charles Carroll of Carrollton, Robert Alexander, Charles Carroll Barrister and James Hollyday. Endorsed "Ballot paper No. 5."

(34 II, 16) Aug. 14(?), 1775 - [Convention of Maryland.]
    Tally of votes for members of the Countil of Safety as follows: Tilghman 16, Johnson 16, Chase 13, Paca 16, Goldsborough 16, Stone 15, Hollyday 15, Carroll Barrister 16, Carroll of Carrollton 10, etc. Endorsed "Ballot Paper No. 3."

(35 II, 27) Aug. 14(?), 1775 - [Convention of Maryland]
    Report of election for Council of Safety; elected for the Western Shore: Thomas Johnson, William Paca, T[homas] Stone, C[harles] Carroll, Barrister, Samuel Chase, D[aniel] of St. T[homas] Jenifer, R[obert]Alexander, C[harles] Carroll of Carrollton. . .

(60 II, 25) 1775 - Account of the Expenses of the Delegates of Maryland to Congress. Lists amounts due to Delegates Thomas Stone, Samuel Chase, William Paca, John Hall and Thomas Johnson.

(75 IV, 151) Jan. 23, 1776 - Daniel of St. Thomas Jenifer, Charles Carroll, John Hall and James Tilghman, Annapolis. To Maryland Deputies, Philadelphia.
    [   ] Maynard is bringing letter from Gov. [Robert] Eden to [   ] Foxcroft, also a letter to [William Legge], Lord Dartmouth; letters were not sent until Matthew Tilghman, Thomas Johnson, Thomas Stone, James Hollyday and the Council were consulted; there is in them no "Intelligence unfriendly to America"; Maynard rates "the proper Passports to New York";

180

postscript says other letters deal with private business from Col. [____] Sim and others to Thomas Eden and Co. Printed in *Archives of Maryland*, XI, 108-109.

(90 IV, 16) Feb. 27, 1776 - Robert Alexander, Phila. To Council of Safety.
Congress has advanced $22,000 (L8,250) to Maryland; cartridge boxes, 25 reams at 16s. per ream, have been purchased; Robert Morris has imported 400 stands of arms and 3,500 pounds of powder for cannon; material will go by stages to Elk, Md., thence by a "back river" to avoid disturbance on the Patapsco; letters smuggled in from Bristol in a barrel of bread; in one was a copy of [Frederick], Lord North's "conciliatory list"; rules for confiscation of trading vessels from January to June are given; "this more than diabolical list" provides for submission of the colonies; "Scotch Junto now disgraces the British Throne"; "Independency" is reprovated but it may be justified by necessity; 26,000 troops are reported as in America; Boston, New York, Virginia, and South Carolina are to be attacked; [Charles], Lord Cornwallis was to sail in January; [Samuel] Chase is going to Canada in a few days; if [John] Rogers absents himself, Maryland will be without representation unless [Thomas] Stone and [Thomas] Johnson should appear; [Matthew] Tilghman has been asked to come; "until a sufft number of my Brothers arrive, I shall not leave this City." Printed in *Archives of Maryland*, XI, 188-190 and in part in *Letters of the Continental Congress*, I, 366-367.

(103 IV, 24) Apr. 2, 1776, Thomas Johnson, Jr., Robert Alexander, William Paca and Thomas Stone, Phila. To Council of Safety.
[Archibald] Buchanan did not take money which [Thomas] Ringgold can bring; L160 17s, 6d. Has been changed to $4,000 for delivery; plates and paper may also go; adjournment of Convention to May 20th is expected; affadavits concerning [Henry(?)] Hudson's ship should be transmitted to get salvage. Signed Johnson, Alexander, Paca, Stone. Printed in *Archives of Maryland*, XI, 306

(106 IV, 26) Apr. 9, 1776, Thomas Johnson, Thomas Stone, and Robert Alexander, Philadelphia. To [Council of Safety].
Thomas Reed, bearer of letter, will also deliver 51 reams of paper; [David] Rittenhouse promises plates [for printing money] by April 13; they will come by post of "some Safe Hand."

(107 IV, 27) Apr. 12, 1776, Thomas Johnson and Thomas Stone, Philadelphia. To [Council of Safety].
Letter of April 9 has just been delivered; enclosed packet was given president; South Carolina sent the packet containing parliamentary act in restraint of Colonial trade passed December, 1775; a ton of powder has been borrowed from Congress for use of Maryland troops; it will be sent to Chestertown, [Maryland]. Printed in *Archives of Maryland*, XI, 328 and *Letters of the Continental Congress*, I, 419.

181

(108 IV, 25) April 13, 1776, Thomas Johnson, Jr., Thomas Stone and Robert Alexander, Philadelphia. To [Council of Safety].

No light duck in Philadelphia to fill recent request; good tenting material can be procured from [David(?)] Bowley; asks about cargo of *Wild Dick;* [Abraham] van Bebber should have written by now; "No important occurrence since we last wrote You"; postscript signed by Robert Alexander asks if "Cruger" can be used for tents. L. Signed "Th. Johnson Junr. T. Stone." Printed in *Archives of Maryland*, XI, 331-332

(116 I, 30) Apr. 17, 1776, Thomas Johnson, Jr., Philadelphia. To Council of Safety.

On April 16, letters arrived from Baltimore; anonymous letter came "under the same Cover"; "Mr. Purviance being the Heroe of the Tale which was told" revealed the authorship of the letter; Andrew Allen knows Purviance's handwriting and "says it was his"; Gen. [Charles] Lee was led to believe Maryland Council of Safety was "timorous and inactive"; the letter was "a vile injurious Calumny calculated . . . to spread Suspicion and Mistrust"; motion to send letter to Council of Safety was put off; [Thomas] Stone and [Robert] Alexander were delayed in attending Congress; heard part of the proceedings and "are, as well as myself, privy to the after Transactions." Printed in *Archives of Maryland*, XI, 347-348 and in *Letters of the Continental Congress*, I, 425-426.

(117 IV, 29) Apr. 18, 1776, Robert Alexander and Thomas Stone, Philadelphia. To [Council of Safety].

Powder has been sent to Chestertown, [Maryland] by wagon; Maj. [Samuel] Smith of [_____] Haines is to receive it; Congress granted this material because of "exposed defences of the Eastern Shore"; part of plates "with the Devices" are sent; [David(?)] Rittenhouse promises rest by April 30.

(118 I, 29) Apr. 18, 1776, Thomas Johnson, Thomas Stone, and Robert Alexander, Philadelphia. To [Council of Safety].

Purviance's letter, by Resolve of Congress, is to be transmitted to Maryland Council of Safety; several hours' debate preceded passage of Resolution; the argument in favor was that "if there rested a suspicion that any publick Body . . . refused to execute the trust committed to them it ought to be made Known to their Constituents"; against the motion was the argument "mischief . . . would be produced by communicating the Letter"; five colonies voted not to request the President to lay the letter before Congress, three voted in the affirmative, and one was divided; on April 17 the "Obligation to Secrecy expired"; [John] Hancock refused to see Maryland delegation; steps to vindicate honor of the Council of Safety should be taken "against the foul Calumny of Mr. Purvyance who has dared to detract from your Patriotism & Spirits"; [Robert} Eden should be secured, along with his papers; further word will come by "Post." Printed in *Archives of Maryland*, XI, 351-352 and *Letters of the Continental Congress*, I, 427-428.

(122 I, 28) Apr. 23, 1776, Thomas Johnson, Jr., Philadelphia. To Daniel of St. Thomas Jenifer, Annapolis.

Word was to be sent by [Charles] Wallace and [Frederick] Green but as post may be swifter, notice of approval of Council of Safety is being sent; "letter to the President gave high offense to some of the very hot Gent."; a resolution may be formed tomorrow; R.A. [Robert Alexander] and T.S. [Thomas Stone] also send respects; reverse: order, partly completed then scored out, to John Gordon for L495 4s. Paid by Treasurer of the Western Shore. Printed in *Archives of Maryland*, XI, 372 and in part in *Letters of the Continental Congress*, I, 429

(134 I, 27) Apr. 24, 1776, T[homas] Stone, Philadelphia. To Daniel of St. Thomas Jenifer, Annapolis.

[Thomas] Johnson wrote Jenifer April 23, 1776; "affairs of Canada" have occupied much time and will continue to do so; "everything will be left to the Convention," as far as the letter is concerned; Gov. [Robert] Eden's letter has been published in a Philadelphia newspaper; soon all governors must quit; quick movements are not wise; peace "on terms of Security and Justice to America" is wanted "but War, anything is preferable to a Surrender of our Rights"; the Maryland Council of Safety has stood for public good and has been "steady firm and determined in . . . opposition to ministerial Tyranny"; on April 27 or 28, Stone expects to meet his wife. Printed in *Archives of Maryland*, XI, 383-384 and in part in *Letters of the Continental Congress*, I, 431-432

(135 I, 31) Apr. 25, 1776, Mat[hew] Tilghman, Thomas Johnson, Jr. and Thomas Stone, Philadelphia. To [Council of Safety].

Letter of April 22 just received; "no fuller proceeding in Congress on Mr. Eden's affair"; [____] King has just been discharged and is therefore not blameworthy; [John} Rogers "should be at the Convention; we don't think the province ought to be left unrepresented here." Printed in *Archives of Maryland*, XI, 386 and in part in *Letters of the Continental Congress*, I, 432.

(150 IV, 30) June 11, 1776, Mathew Tilghman, Thomas Stone, and John Rogers, Philadelphia. To Council of Safety.

[Charles(?)] Steward brought a letter from Council and by the post a letter dated June 7; [Robert] Morris has recommended men to fit out gallies; arms lent by Congress are unavailable; Maryland is thought to be inaccessible to attack; flying camp quota is 3,400 men, as inclosed resolve shows; Virginia has given 'an ungenerous and malevolent Turn" to Maryland proceedings; apparently they wish to "stir up the People of Maryland against their Representatives"; debate on independence will be resumed in 3 weeks; Convention of Maryland must decide this and notify Congressional deputies; latter would attend Convention if necessary; whether harvesting prevents or not, Convention must be held; proceedings of last session of the Convention should be sent to Philadelphia; King and ministers won't offer terms acceptable to America; [Samuel] Smith's reports about Capt. [____] Hammond and [John], Lord Dunmore do not indicate peace; gun carriage, instruments, and paper will be sent. L. Signed by Matthew Tilghman, Thomas Stone and John Rogers. Printed in *Archives of Maryland*, XI, 477-479; in part in *Letters of the Continental Congress*, I, 485-486.

(154 IV, 32) June 15, 1776, Thomas Stone, [John] Rogers, Philadelphia. To [Council of Safety].
    Acknowledges letter of June 10; militia cannot be ordered from Province by Congress; "flying camps" are to accept volunteer militia for defense of Middle Colonies; delegates can hardly be expected to attend Convention and neglect Congressional duties; [Matthew] Tilghman has left; British and American cannon differ in weight; postscript mentions articles sent by stage. L. Signed: "T. Stone, Rogers." Printed in *Archives of Maryland*, XI, 492-493; in *Letters of the Continental Congress*, I, 492-493.

(157 II, 145) June [21] 1776, Convention of Maryland. List of members: from Charles County: Josias Hawkins, Robert T[ownsend] Hooe, T[homas] Stone, J[oseph] H. Harrison, William Harrison.

(214 IV, 33) July 4, 1776, Receipt for order on Continental Congress.
    Acknowledges receipt of order for $5,000 for use of Maryland Council of Safety in recruiting from German companies. D. Signed: "Wm. Paca, J. Rogers, T. Stone"
    Endorsed twice in a later hand: "This is a very valuable paper, showing who were the **three required** representatives of Maryland **present in Congress**, between the 1 and 4 July 1776, **who voted for Independence.** Brantz Mayer" and "The within paper should be preserved with great care as it's the best document possessed by the State showing who were the 3 representatives of Maryland **present in Congress at Philad.** on the 4th of July 1776. Brantz Mayer

(254 IV, 35) July 22, 1776, Thomas Stone and William Paca, Philadelphia. To [Council of Safety]
    Congress has granted $5,000 to Maryland to raise 4 German companies; the dollars will be exchanged for "Maryland Convention money"; account is inclosed; [Daniel] Hughes changed the money; Lt. Col. [George] Stricker has been appointed to the German battalions; he is now in Frederick County, [Maryland] where $1,520 should be sent for expenses; Col. [Francis] Ware and Maj. [Mordecai] Gist have been given L82 10s.; postscript says mention of $2,000 in a previous letter was a mistake. Printed in *Archives of Maryland*, XII, 93-94 and in *Letters of the Continental Congress*, VII, 24.

(255 IV, 36) July 23, 1776, Samuel Chase and Thomas Stone, Philadelphia. To Council of Safety.
    Acknowledge letter of July 19; letters of Cols. [Richard] Barnes and

184

[Jeremiah] Jordan were not sent; Capts. [John Allen] Thomas and James Hindman should go to "flying camp"; Gen. Washington has only 5,000 troops; men without arms are useless; inclosed are terms obtained from expert in refinig sulphur; no news has come yet of [Richard], Lord Howe's fleet Printed in *Archives of Maryland*, XII, 105-106..

(257 IV, 37) July 24, 1776, Thomas Stone, Philadelphia. To Council of Safety.
    40 barrels of powder and 54 stand of arms are being sent; each wagoner will get L12; goods will leave Egg Harbor, [New Jersey]; Harrison & van Bebber have a 10% of gross sale; guards will watch powder and arms at 5s. A day; "Nothing since ours by post." Printed in *Archives of Maryland*, XII, 110.

(261 IV, 39) July 30, 1776, Thomas Stone, Philadelphia. To Council of Safety.
    Instruments desired by Maryland may be delayed as "cutlers" have gone to [New] Jersey with the militia; both powder and arms have been sent; Maryland must help "that our Coast will be secured against the Ravages of [John, Lord] Dunmore and his rascally Gang of Pirates"; enemy is still on Staten Island, [New York], 8 ships having joined them there; Washington has strength in New York but only 3,000 men in [New] Jersey; Col. [William] Smallwood is also in New York; hunting shirts would make good uniforms; postscript states that his "brothers" are too busy to sign. Printed in *Archives of Maryland*, XII, 146-147.

(264 IV, 40) Aug. 13, 1776, Thomas Stone, Philadelphia. To Council of Safety.
    Pleased that [John, Lord] Dunmore's fleet has left the Chesapeake; Capt. [John?] Thomas' company has arrived; hopes to see Capt. [Charles] Griffith shortly; difficulties of recruitment for Flying Camp are appreciated; 15,000 British troops are now on Staten Island, [New York]; Washington moved 2,000 men from [New] Jersey to York, [Pennsylvania]; is leaving Philadelphia on August 20. Printed in *Archives of Maryland*, XII, 199-200.

(284 IV, 42) Sept. 20, 1776, Thomas Johnson, Jr., William Paca, Samuel Chase, Thomas Stone, Philadelphia. To Council of Safety.
    Capt. [Thomas] Watkins will report to Council only 37 effectives in his company; desertions are due to lack of clothing and blankets; Lt. [Solomon(?)] Long has gone to Worcester County to induce deserters to return; Capt. [John Allen(?)] Thomas reports that sick soldiers have no proper care; Dr. [____] Bond has tried to get a suitable person for the Independent companies but without success; Gen. Washington's report of September 18 indicates 100 British killed in skirmish on September 16; Maj. [____] Leach of Virginia was wounded; [William] Richardson's and [Charles Greenbury] Griffith's battalions were in the action; general attack was later made on Washington's lines; Col. Richardson reports Capt. Watkins "addicted to Drink." Printed in *Archives of Maryland*, XII, 291-292.

(298 IV, 44) Oct. 24, 1776, Benjamin Rumsey, Philadelphia. To James Tilghman, [Annapolis].

He arrived October 19 and other Maryland delegates October 21; placed Resolves before Congress on October 22; the Maryland plan to substitute $10 for 100 acres of land was declared by Congress one which "would break the Back of all North America"; Maryland thinks "ten Dollars now" better than "trust to the Mercy of a few Venders" who would raise prices; Maryland has no land; [John] Dickinson, [Thomas] McKean, [James] Wilson, [Benjamin] Rush represent the "Aristocraticks"; Ens. Valentine Creager, Philip Smith, Lt. George Need, Ens. John Perkinson are officers of Frederick County flying camp; roll sent Maj. [Daniel of St. Thomas] Jenifer was dated Sept. 19, 1776; commissions are still lacking although [Adam] Fisher, Col. [John] Stull and [Thomas] Stone have been asked; enlisted men of camp are leaving for other regiments; Gabriel Duvall had said commissions were in Philadelphia; John Hancock said they were in Maryland; a4 German companies formed in Maryland complain of 5 German companies from Pennsylvania; [William] Smallwood is a brigadier; postscript mentions that militia from [New] Jersey "have so frightened the Common People that none will enlist." Printed in *Archives of Maryland*, XII, 397-400

(324 III, 3) Nov. 10, 1776, [Convention of Maryland]

Resolution, adopted upon considering the letter from Congress of October 2, appointing Matthew Tilghman, Thomas Johnson, Jr., William Paca, Thomas Stone, Samuel Chase, Benjamin Rumsey and Charles Carroll, Barrister, to be Delegates to Congress and authorizing them to concur with the other states in forming a confederation and making foreign alliances subject to the assent of the General Assembly; they are also authorized to concur in other measures for prosecuting the war, reserving to the State the sole right of regulating its internal police, and to concur with Congress in accommodating the differences with Great Britain. Printed in *Convention Proceedings*, 373-374.

(352 IV, 57) Dec. 24, 1776, Samuel Chase, Strawberry Mount, [Maryland]. To Council of Safety

Account delivered is thought just; [Thomas] Stone ordered clothes for Capt. [Thomas] Watkins' Company; lack of cash prevented payment. Printed in *Archives of Maryland*, XII, 552

(477 IV, 81) Dec. 9, 1777, Thomas Stone, Portobacco, [Maryland]. To Gov. Thomas Johnson.

Phoenix and *Emerald*, British ships are in the Potomac; Capt. Hyde Parkin(?) Has issued a manifesto offering to buy provisions or seize them; "fugitive Negroes" have given them some help; pillaging is now expected; even with arms, repelling a landing may be impossible; 100 marines are on these ships; needed arms can "be returned whenever the occasion for them ceases."

(478 IV, 83) Thomas Stone, Portobacco [Maryland]. To Thomas Sim Lee.

Lt. [James] Smith brought supplies from Council; British ships lie opposite Upper Cedar Point, [Maryland]; militia is prepared at all invation points; a "thieving party" was taken near Sandy Point, [Maryland]; Col. [Francis] Ware exchanged prisoner for "an American Master" held on the Phoenix; Ware is now in Picawaxent (?); no provisions from the county can be obtained by the British.

(479 IV, 84) Thomas Stone, "Charles County," [Maryland] To [Governor and Council.]

Enemy is between Boyd's Hob and Nanjemoy; if Virginia and Maryland could jointly attack, the British ships might flee; their *Phoenix* has run aground "more than once"; Col. [Francis] Ware has served well as county lieutenant.

(1106 IV, 117) Apr. 17, 1781, Thomas Stone, Portobacco, [Maryland]. To Gov. [Thomas Sim] Lee.

Brig with 16 guns was seen off Swan Point, [Maryland]; 8 militia under Col. [____] Harris repulsed a landing party; enemy fleet sailed down the Potomac Bay and Cedar Point, [Maryland]; Col [____] Lyle's house was destroyed; arms to repel the "plundering Banditti" are needed. Printed in *Archives of Maryland*, XLVII, 197-198.

(1108 III, 24) Apr. 18, 1781, T[homas] Stone, [Portobacco, Maryland]. To [Thomas Johnson, Jr.]

On April 12, 1781 British vessels landed marauders at "Portobacco" and stole church furnishings; on April 13 the enemy landed at Capt. George Dent's and burned the houses; Cedar Point, [Maryland] was robbed of tobacco on April 14; 5 or 6 barges and 300 men were in the invasion; to defend all points, arms are needed; 2 or 3 cannons are needed; "public tobacco" should be moved; British vessels rounded Cedar Point April 17, and are anchored at Swan Point [Maryland]; Col. [Francis] Ware cannot give account of transactions.

Copy. Annotated p.3 "The original of this letter sent to the Reverend Jared Sparks of Boston, by permission of the Executive, to be inserted in a Volume of FacSimiles, which the said Sparks designs to publish, of Letters of distinguished Revolutionary Characters. By Tho: Culbreth, Clerk of the Council." [1826?]

CALENDAR OF MARYLAND STATE PAPERS
The Red Books
Number 4, Part 2

(425 XV, 20) July 27, 1776, Samuel Chase and Charles Carroll of Carrollton, Philadelphia. To Council of Safety.

Have advanced Col. [William] Smallwood $1,335; Smallwood recommends that Christopher Richmond be appointed regimental paymaster for his battalion; the fifty muskets lodged in [Thomas] Stone's house could be kept there to arm State militia passing through Philadelphia to the flyhing camp; large quantities of flint-stones are reported at the landings on Wye and Choptank Rivers, where they were discarded after serving as ballast; Gen. Washington reports all quiet. Printed in *Archives of Maryland*, XII, 129-130.

(797 XIII, 123) Dec. 14, 1776, Amos Taylor, Philadelphia. To Samuel Chase and William Paca, Baltimore.

George Fox is sent with letter and bills for clothing, (Capt [Thomas] Watkin's company); bills had been presented December 7; Lt. Richard Grace and Thomas Stone can testify as to delivery; [Michael] Hillegas has been notified; "a couple of Poor Tradesmen" need the money.

(1488 XX, 70) Feb. 2, 1778, Account of Clothing Purchased in Charles County by Daniel Jenifer.

Lists clothing obtained from the following persons: . . . Mary Stone, Richard Stone, Thomas Stone . . .

CALENDAR OF MARYLAND STATE PAPERS
No. 5 Executive Miscellanea

(224 Exec. Papers Box I, 19) Dec. 7, 1775, [Convention of Maryland]

List of members by counties: Charles: William Smallwood, Francis Ware, Josias Hawkins, Robert T[ownsend] Hooe, Thomas Stone

(352 Red Book IV, 175) [June 8, 1776] Council of Safety. To Deputies of Maryland in Congress, [Philadelphia].

[Thomas] Stone's letter of June 4 has been received and the Deputies have no doubt received the Council's letter by [Stephen] Steward; Gov. [Robert Eden] is leaving soon and onlyh time will tell whether the Virginians will interfere with his passage down the Bay; the Virginia resolutions, which came addressed to Charles Carroll, [Barrister], Chairman of the Convention, are clearly intended to stir up the people of Maryland against those who govern them; if Congress requests that the militia be marched, the Convention must be called; 3,400 militia would take all serviceable arms, leaving the Province an easy prey for enemy ships and the ministerial troops; [Samuel] Purviance "got off with a severe Reprimand." Printed in *Archives of Maryland*, XI, 470-471.

(632, Exec. Papers, Box VII, 7) March 26, 1776, Governor and Council.

Order directing Dr. [Richard] Tootle to deliver to Thomas Stone "one pound of Jallop for the use of some people who are under Innoculation in Charles County." Printed in *Archives. of Maryland*, XVI, 189 with Tootle's name spelled, "Tooth."

(688 Exec. Papers, Box VII, 51) April 18, 1777, Bond of Whittey Turpin, To State of Maryland.

  The condition is that Turpin be of good behavior during the war. D.S. Also signed by William Adams, Henry Jackson and Samuel Wilson as securities and by J[oseph] Nicholson, Jr. and T[homas] Stone as witnesses. (898 Blue Book, V. 38) [Mar. 27], 1778, Oath of Allegiance, Charles County, Richard Barnes' Return. The oath of allegiance in full is on page one; pages two, three, four, and five contain the following names, including the name of Thomas Stone.

Addendum A
Family Correspondence

The James Monroe-Thomas Stone family connection was based on Philadelphia society about 1791 during a visit of the Stone daughters to their uncle and guardian, Congressman Michael Jenifer Stone. His position in the Capital's social warp and weave brought the Stone girls of Habre de Venture into intimate contact with those closely associated with those who were prominent in Philadelphia society as well as those connected with the First Congress of the United States. An interesting part of Margaret's letter to uncle Walter Jenifer Stone in Port Tobacco was her reference to mutual friends whom Walter had known when he was employed in the Nation's Capital a few years earlier:

My dear Uncle,

You are much surprised no doubt that I have not written before this - which I know always has its full weight with you so you shall hear the cause. When we first arrived here we were in the midst of confusion, not getting our cloaths and all such <u>important nothings</u> - well I waited till I cou'd tell you how agreeably we were fix't, how many, many visitors we had - how delighted we were with ourselves and everybody - but behold just as I's begun my _____ my eyes got in a vehement passion, were so violently red that I was confined eight days to a room as dark as a dungeon, which to be sure was dismal enough. I bore it all with <u>common</u> patience and blessed the day I was released - with a determination the first thing I did was to be scribble a way to you, but when I got down stairs there was so many congratulations, visitations, and invitations that this is the first moment I have had the command of for a week – which is humbly devoted to you, you see - we are most charmingly fix't. Mr. Bend is a polite clever man. Mrs. Bend (who is niece to Mrs. Stockton) is extremely friendly <u>really a Lady</u> – Colonel Monroe *very fond of us all, Mrs. Monroe very unreserved and friendly – she's agreeable, sensible and thought the prettiest woman in Philadelphia – she's among the prettiest I ever saw – F.S. has been to see us. A. Scott visits us often and much improved – Fred has grown monstrously fat and all that's clever. If you were with us we should be quite happy. "Philadelphia is one dandy." We were at the Levee Friday last, everyone very fine making their congees* [to take one's leave], *the President honored by speaking to us very often, we were invited to a grand rout* [a fashionable assembly, a large evening party] *at _____ next Tuesday; we din'd at Dr. Rush's* [Benjamin] *on Christmas Day. He calls us his nieces, says he must have an equal right with Uncle M.J.S. for he says he must give up one to him he says, too. His friendship is on account of the S. family but his affection is on Uncle D*[aniel']*s account. All yr old acquaintances enquire a great deal for you, particularly the Miss Pettit and Mrs. Stockton and daughter. Mr. Morris visited us to apologize for Mrs. Morris – her mother died 4 days ago, that with her illness has prevented our seeing Mrs. M. I have not seen Miss Footman, Miss Francis or the Miss Allen any where. Miss Turner was married to Mr. Miller soon after we arrived, so that chance for the great fortune is gone to you – you never counted much on it though. The smartest beau here is a South Carolinian - he is very witty much in the style of Ned Jones - but handsome beyond compare. He gallants* [escorts] *by turns every young lady here. He attended us to* [two] *at the Levee* [one of the President's receptions]. *Mr. Sumter is all the <u>Ton</u>* [style, fashion] *with men, women and children. Uncle M* [Congressman Michael Jenifer Stone] *says he's a <u>wonder</u>. I shall write you a d— next week. I'm called of just now. Give my love to all friends. Milly desires hers. Our French's not well*

191

*has been bad but we do tolerably well and live in
hopes.*

Yours affectionately,
Margaret Stone

Philadelphia, Jan. 9, 1791

The letter below from a quite young Mrs. James Monroe addressed to Habre de Venture indicates the Stones were part of our new Nation's high society. James, from northern Virginia, married 17-year old Elizabeth Kortright, daughter of a New York City merchant. Michael Jenifer Stone, serving in New York City during the First U.S. Congress, had been visited by his nieces from Port Tobacco. Apparently they met the young Mrs. Monroe in New York. Michael Jenifer Stone served in Congress until March 1791. Now, with the seat of government in Philadelphia and her husband still a part of it, Eliza wrote to Margaret, still at Habre de Venture. One hopes the two young women ultimately did greet each other at Habre de Venture. The authors furnished the detailed attribution for this Monroe letter, which had been given to the Rappahannock Regional Library, Fredericksburg, Virginia by a direct Stone descendant, about 1983. When Eliza Monroe died her husband destroyed all of her personal papers. The Eliza letter to Habre de Venture was a rare discovery and a notable contribution to the James Monroe Museum in Fredericksburg, Virginia. A letter written and signed by Eliza Monroe is a treasure, the more so to us because of to whom it was sent:

Philadelphia, March 15, 1792 [Mildred apparently not at Habre de Venture now – no doubt married and in Virginia with husband Travers Daniel, Jr. Addressed to Miss Margaret Stone at Habre de Venture from Mrs. Eliza Monroe (Mrs. James Monroe of Virginia)].

> *I must apologize my dear Margaret for not
> having earlier answered your very friendly letter. You
> will have the kindness to attribute it to a thousand
> little engagements which take ones attention in such
> a place as this from objects infinitely more
> interesting. I accept with the greatest pleasure your
> proposal for correspondence in future, and will
> endeavor to give you whatever passes within my view
> that may amuse you. But as it will be formed on the*

most sincere and mutual friendship, it contains nothing more than an occasional account of our welfare and that of our friends, it would be a sufficient inducement with both.

We have missed you all much this winter—our house is at the extremity of Arch Street at a distance from our acquaintance and almost out of the world. Had you been with us we should have been in every respect more comfortable than we then were . . . for in Mr. M's [Monroe] *and Uncle Michael's* [Congressman Michael J. Stone left Congress in March 1791, after serving only one term] *absence we co's we could have kept up each others spirits, which is difficult for me to do when quite alone. I have not entered much into the gayiety of the place this winter – those parties I have attended were very brilliant and the dress of the ladies generally more costly than they were the last. Indeed everything has put on a more extravagant appearance. Many strangers have been here from every quarter. Among those Mr. and Miss Ogle from Maryland. I doubt not they were much pleased, they were so much taken up with the round of amusements, that I had not opportunity of any private conversation with them.*

I staid abt. 7 weeks with my friends in New York upon my first arrival. When last I heard from them they were well.

When we set out for Virginia is uncertain but presume it will be sometime in April. I look forward to it with pleasure, as Mr. M. has promised me if possible to stay a day or two at Haberdeventure. I shall write you again and hope to hear from you before that time; say everything that friendship dictates to Milly and Uncle Michael, and tell them that nothing . . . shall prevent my seeing them soom. Mr. Monroe and dear Eliza [very young Monroe daughter] *join me in love to you all. Believe me my dear Margaret there is not one among your friends*

that wishes more sincerely for your happiness than
yours affectionately . . . E. Monroe

A letter written by a much younger Margaret in 1782, again
to her Uncle Watty in Philadelphia, reveals a childish humor;

Habredeventure May 3d 1782,
Dear Uncle–I take this opportunity of letting you see I
have not forgot you and must inform you that I most
ardently wish for your return. It seems like Six Years
since your departure.

> *I immagine Philadelphia is very agreeable to*
> *you as it Is a gay Place, I shou'd be much obliged to*
> *you if you wou'd inform Me how the little Girls of my*
> *Age dress and Please to present my Compliments to*
> *the Miss Bonds and Miss Meads If they Are in the*
> *City. Mama, I think is better than she has Been for*
> *some time–Aunt Scott I believe is mending very*
> *fast–Both my Aunt Edens are well and Aunt Stone has*
> *a Son–Miss Mosbyn is at Dr. Balls and has been there*
> *for some time–Cousin Sally, Milly and Frederick*
> *desire their love to their Dr. Uncle Wat. I wish you a*
> *great deal of Health and Happiness–I am, Dr. Uncle*
> *Your most Effectionate Niece, Margaret Stone. P.S.*
> *Mama wou'd be obliged to you if you wou'd get her*
> *two Pound of Cream of Tartar. She takes it in large*
> *quantity's–she wou'd send the Cash To procure it but*
> *Papa is not At Home. Please to send it by Mr. Jack*
> *Brown.*

A December 3, 1783 letter from Thomas to brother Walter
(Watty, as always) fleshes out the Stone lives at this time. This letter
reflects Stone as father, husband and brother and reveals some of the
intimate, innermost facets of his character. Oddly, the Stones seem
now to be at Habre de Venture rather than the Peggy Stewart house
in the State capital. And Walter now is staying in Annapolis and
seems concerned about his soon-to-be life as a merchant in Port
Tobacco. His days as a government clerk have ended. He desired on-
the-job training at some business house in Baltimore, but Thomas
advises against it, saying

Letter from Thomas to brother Walter in Philadelphia who as a government employee doubtless performed many errands for Thomas, now at Habre de Venture, but asking favors for the Washington family.

New York Public Library

> *. . it will be of no advantage to you . . . can't you acquire as much knowledge at Annapolis . . . you want steadiness [of] thought and attention more than knowledge and I am sure Baltimore is not the place to acquire these habits – time and proper reflection will be the best instructions . . . God grant that they may have their proper influence.*

And, at this time at Habre de Venture Thomas is in serious need of his carriage left in Annapolis (apparently not the one made in Philadelphia in 1776). So, he sends servants Webster and Jack to get this conveyance from Walter along with some clothes from a trunk

> *and take care not to throw out any papers.*

Also,

> *I want the carriage daily, being extremely low [ill] and requiring exercise.*

Stone also writes to Watty

> *. . . Both Mrs. Stone and myself are very sick and she must have a disagreeable time here . . . we are obliged to keep as free from company as possible – the children are also very sickly.*

Then,

> *If I should be better and Mrs. Stone's health is tolerable we shall spend [the remainder] of the winter in Annapolis . . . at present neither of us can move out . . . I have been writing all morning and am now so fatigued that I must conclude and lie down.*

One must assume Stone at Habre de Venture had no clerical assistance. [165]

About a week later Thomas informed Walter in Annapolis that the carriage and articles sent down to Port Tobacco had arrived without damage. He comments

> *. . . this is by no means so good a carriage as I expected for the money, and the want of safe brakes is material, but men will not be honest, and there is no help for it.*

---

165 Columbia University Rare Book and Manuscript Library, New York, NY. Letter from Thomas Stone to brother Walter, December 3, 1783.

Again, about Walter's education in the affairs of commerce, Thomas wrote

> . . . *I wish you to pursue whatever course of life promises the fairest chance of final success upon a consideration of all circumstances and shall at all times give you my advice with the sincerity and freedom becoming a brother. The major* [Daniel of St. Thomas Jenifer] *and Co.* [John H. Stone] *will be good judges what is for your advantage . . . I am mending fast and think and hope to be at Annapolis in a week or ten days . . .*

In this letter Stone discusses a current effort in Charles County to move the county seat of Charlestown (popularly called Port Tobacco) to some point about three to four miles away to a point more easily reached by vessels. Not until 1896 did this come about and at this time the cause of removal was a steam engine and rail system rather than a sea and ship method of transporting tobacco, which until nearly the 21st century remained the major cash crop of most of southern Maryland.

Finally, Thomas tells Walter he had just given refuge to young local lawyer William Craik, the oldest son of Revolutionary War Surgeon General James Craik. Dr. Craik lived near Port Tobacco from 1762 until he moved to Alexandria, Virginia (at the suggestion of George Washington) in 1783. This move of the Craiks from their home La Grange seems to have left young William without a local domicile. Thomas wrote

> . . . *Mr. William Craik has just come to live with me. I could not refuse this pressing solicitation, as he is a very worthy young man.*

In December 1799 Dr. James Craik was one of three physicians at Washington's bedside when he died. [166]

The above letters from Stone reveal a remarkable human being having normal frailties, love of family and respect for friends and neighbors as well as dissatisfaction with life's setbacks and losses

---

166   Columbia University Rare Book and Manuscript Library, New York, NY. Letter from Thomas Stone to brother Walter from Habre de Venture December 9, 1783.

common to us all. Reflections of Stone as father, brother and neighbor dovetail nicely into our perception of the man founded on his contributions as patriot, legislator, rebel with cause and lawyer. He was a respected peer of many of the most illustrious figures in the magnificent panorama of events leading to our new nation in 1776. Stone's humility, warmth and sensitivity for the needs of others may have been in part a reason for his incredible obscurity during the past two centuries.

Addendum B
Bibliography

Charles Francis Adams, Ed., *Adams Papers, Works of John Adams.*

American Archives, 4th series, v.1.

Matthew Page Andrews, *Tercentenary History of Maryland,* (Chicago-
    Baltimore: S.J. Clark Publishing Co., Vol. I, 1925.)

Archives of Maryland.

Archives of Maryland, Maryland Hall of Records, Annapolis, MD., Charles
    County Chancery Court records, No. 4647, Nov. 30, 1808.

Archives of Maryland, Maryland Hall of Records, Annapolis, MD., Charles
    County Chancery Court records, No. 4818, Daniel of St. Thomas
    Jenifer, 30 May 1783.

Archives of Maryland, Maryland Hall of Records, Annapolis, MD., Charles
    County Court Proceedings, 1826-1829.

Archives of Maryland, Maryland Hall of Records, Annapolis, MD., Charles
    County Land Records, Liber S3.

Archives of Maryland, Maryland Hall of Records, Annapolis, MD., Charles
    County Rent Roll, Liber 5, F. 322, 1685.

Archives of Maryland, Maryland Hall of Records, Annapolis, MD., Charles
    County 1783 Tax Assessment Records.

Archives of Maryland, Maryland Hall of Records, Annapolis, MD., Charles
    County Register of Wills, Thomas Stone will, Liber AH7..

Henry Buckle, *History of Civilization in England,* London   Edition, 1857.

E. C. Burnett, *Letters of Members of the Continental Congress,* Vol.   VII.

L. H. Butterfield, Ed., *John Adams Diary and Autobiography.* Vol. 2,
    Harvard University Press.

College of Southern Maryland, Southern Maryland Studies Center, oral history
    taped interview with Lorena Butler Chambers by John M. Wearmouth,
    1985.

Columbia University Rare Book and Manuscript Library, New York, NY.

Congressional Record, May 10, 1978 and October 12, 1978.

Alan F. Day dissertation, *A Social Study of Lawyers in Maryland, 1660-1775.*
    University of Edinburgh. Maryland Hall of Records, Annapolis,
    Maryland.

Ron Deiss, *Archaeological Excavations at the Thomas Stone Historic Site,*
    1986, Port Tobacco, Maryland.

Edward S. Delaplaine, *The Life of Thomas Johnson.* (New York: Hitchcock
    Publishing Co., Grafton Press, 1927).

Malone Dumas, Ed., *Dictionary of American Biography.* Under the auspices of
    The American Council of Learned Societies, 9 volumes. (New York:
    Scribner's 1936).

D.S. & V.I. Eaton, "The Dye is Cast," *The Library of Congress Quarterly
    Journal of Current Acquisitions,* Vol. 14, number 4 (Aug. 1957).

Thomas Addis Emmet Collection, 1483-1876 Manuscripts and Archives
Division, New York Public Library, New York, NY. Letter written by
Thomas Stone with engraving of house.

John Fiske, *Critical Period of American History,* (New York and Boston:
Houghton, Mifflin Co., 1886).

John S. H. Fogg, Autograph Collection, Maine Historical Society, Portland,
Maine.

.George Forbes Collection, *Record of Forensic Club Meetings and
Membership, 1759-1767,* Archives of Maryland, Maryland
Hall of Records, Annapolis, MD MSA SC4389, ms.

The Formation of the Union, National Archives Publication #7013.
(General Services Administration, Washington, DC, 1970)

Richard Frothingham, *The Rise of the Republic of the United States,* Tenth
Edition, Boston: Little, Brown and Company, 1910.

General Services Administration, National Archives and Records
Service, *Papers of the Continental Congress, 1771-1789,*
Washington, DC., Microfilm Rolls 9, 22, 61 and 68 (84).

Gratz Autograph Collection, Historical Society of Pennsylvania, Philadelphia.
Folio p.1.s., case 1, box 11. Letter from Thomas Stone to George Washington,
January 28, 1785.

Horace Edwin Hayden, *Virginia Genealogies, Brown family portion.*
Baltimore, Maryland: Baltimore Genealogical Publishing Co., Inc.,
1979 (reprint).

Inventory, David Stone's estate.

House Journal, February session 1777, pp. 50-51.

Donald Jackson & Dorothy Twohig, Eds., *The Diaries of George Washington,*
Vol. IV, March 20, 1785. University Press of Virginia,
Charlottesville, 1978.

Sonia Johnston, *American Paintings, 1750-1900,* Baltimore, MD

Journals of the Continental Congress, U.S. National Archives and
Records Service, Washington, DC.

Ross M. Kimmel, *Perspective: William Smallwood,* Maryland Park Service,
Department of Natural Resources, Annapolis, MD: 1976.

Frank Willing Leach, *Genealogy of the Signers of the Declaration of
Independence.* Unpublished manuscript, c.1886.

Library of Congress, *Letters of Delegates to Congress, 1774-1789,*
Vol. 4, (Government Printing Office, Washington, DC, 1979)

Library of Congress, Manuscript Division. Letter from Thomas Stone to
George Washington, January 30, 1787 and February 16, 1787.
George Washington letter to The Honorable Charles Carroll and The
Honorable Thomas Stone, December 3, 1785.

Library of Congress, Manuscript Division, *Stone Family of Maryland*
collection.

Maryland Gazette, Annapolis, Maryland, March 2, 1769, November 4, 1784,
August 10, 1786 and December 28, 1786.

Maryland Hall of Records, Patents & Tracts.

Maryland Historical Magazine, "The Founding of St. John's College," Baltimore, June 1949.

Maryland Historical Society, Baltimore, MD, Letter of Thomas Stone to [Charles Carroll of Annapolis] [May? 1776] used as a wrapper, MdHI, MS 206.

Maryland Historical Society, Baltimore, MD, MS 406, *Stone Family Correspondence.*

Maryland Historical Society, Baltimore, MD, MS 1303.

The Maryland Society of the Sons of the American Revolution, *The Maryland Signers of the Declaration of Independence – Their Homes and Places of Burial. 1912.*

Lillian B. Miller, *The Dye is Now Cast. The Road to American Independence 1774-1776.* Published for the National Portrait Gallery by the Smithsonian Press: Washington, D.C., 1975.

Lynn Montross, *Rag, Tag and Bobtail.* (New York: Harper & Bros., 1952.)

Richard B. Morris, *The Mount Vernon Conference: First Step Toward Philadelphia.* Mount Vernon, Virginia, 1985.

Mount Vernon Ladies' Association of the Union: 1985 Annual Report, Mount Vernon, VA, 1985.

Myers Collection #758, 1 and 2, Rare Books and Manuscript Division, New York Public Library, New York, NY.

National Archives and Records Service, *The Declaration of Independence - A History,* Website: http:www.nars.gov/exhall/charters/declaration/dechist.html.

National Archives Publication #7013, *The Formation of the Union.* (General Services Administration, Washington, D. C., 1970.)

National Journal, Feb. 28, 1826.

National Park Service, U. S. Custom House, Philadelphia, National Historic Landmark File, Office of Cultural Resource Management, Mid-Atlantic Region.

Harry Wright Newman, *The Stones of Poynton Manor* (Washington, DC., published by author, 1937.)

Edward C. Papenfuse, Alan F. Day, David W. Jordan and Gregory A. Stiverson, *A Biographical Dictionary of the Maryland Legislature, 1635-1789,* Vol. 2:I-Z. (Baltimore and London: The Johns Hopkins University Press, 1985.)

Edward C. Papenfuse, Letter from State Archivist (Maryland) and Commissioner of Land Patents to the Honorable William S. James, State Treasurer, Annapolis, June 5, 1986.

Papers of the Continental Congress, Number 32, pp. 127-133, Number 20 I p. 401; Number 36 II, pp. 447, 451.

Park-Bernet Galleries, Inc., 980 Madison Ave., NY, NY. Sale #2569, auction of May 16, 1967, p. 46, Lot 57.

Philip B. Perlman, "Some Lawyers in Supreme Court History," *The Maryland Historical Magazine, Vol. XLIII, No. 3*, Sept. 1948, The Maryland Historical Society, Baltimore, MD.

Henry Fletcher Powell, compiler, *Tercentenary History of Maryland*, Vol. IV. (Chicago-Baltimore: S. J. Clark Publishing Co., 1925.)

Princetonians: A Biographical Dictionary, MS, Firestone Library, Princeton University, Princeton, New Jersey.

Publication 15, Hall of Records, *The Governors of Maryland*, Annapolis, 1970.

Red Books - Parts I and II, Calendar of Maryland State Papers, Hall of Records Commission No. 7, (Annapolis, MD., 1950.)

David C. Roller & Robert W. Twyman, eds., *The Encyclopedia of Southern History*, (Baton Rouge & London: Louisiana State University Press, 1979.)

Kate Mason Rowland, The Letters of Richard Henry Lee, *The Life of George Mason, II.* (New York, The MacMillan Co., 1914.)

John Sanderson, *Biography of the Signers to the Declaration of Independence.* Philadelphia: R. W. Pomeroy, 1824.

J. Thomas Scharf, *A History of Maryland.* Volume 2. (Baltimore MD: 1879.)

St. George L. Sioussat, "The Chevalier de la Luzerne and the Ratification of the Articles of Confederation by Maryland, 1780-1781." Offprint from *The Pennsylvania Magazine of History and Biography*, Philadelphia, October 1936.

Edith Moore Sprouse, *Colchester: Colonial Port on the Potomac*, Fairfax County (Virginia) Office of Comprehensive Planning, Fairfax, Virginia, March 1975, Glassford & Col., Vol. #123, p. 121.

David McNeely Stauffer autograph collection of the Signers of the Declaration of Independence, 1878-1890, Library of Congress, Washington, D. C.

Robert G. Stewart, *Robert Edge Pine: A British Portrait Painter in America*, National Portrait Gallery, Smithsonian Institution Press, Washington: 1979.

Gregory A. Stiverson and Phebe R. Jacobson, *William Paca, A Biography*, (Baltimore: Maryland Historical Society, 1976.) Foreword.

Thomas Stone will.

William Briscoe Stone Collection, William Perkins Library, Special Collections, Duke University, Durham, North Carolina.

Betty Carney Taussig, *Windfall of Inherited Treasures*, Windfall Publishing Co., Annapolis, Maryland, 1983.

Roger Thomas , *Brown Books - No. 3, Calendar of Maryland State Papers*, The Hall of Records Commission No. 6, (Annapolis, MD., 1948.)

U.S. Department of Interior, National Park Service, National Historic Landmarks File, Office of Cultural Resource Management, Mid-Atlantic Region, U.S. Custom House, Philadelphia, PA, "Peggy Stewart House."

Virginia Journal and Alexandria Advertiser, October 11, 1787.

Jean H. Vivian, "Thomas Stone and the Re-organization of the Maryland Council of Safety, 1776." *Maryland Historical Magazine*, volume LXIX (1974).

Votes and Proceedings of the House of Delegates of the State of Maryland - October session, 1781 being the first session of this assembly.

Votes and Proceedings of the Senate of the State of Maryland - October session, 1781 being the first session of this assembly,

Lorena Seebach Walsh, *Charles County, Maryland, 1658-1705: A Study of Chesapeake Political and Social Structure*, (Ph.D. dissertation, Michigan State University, 1977).

Wanamaker Scrapbook, Historical Society of Pennsylvania, Philadelphia.

John M. Wearmouth, *Thomas Stone National Historic Site - Historic Resource Study. Part 1 - Biographical Sketch: Part 2 - Property History: Part 3 - Land Use History: Part 4 - Legislative History*, May 11, 1988.

Roberta J. Wearmouth, *Abstracts from the Port Tobacco Times and Charles County Advertiser, Volume Two: 1855-1869*. (Bowie, Maryland: Heritage Books, Inc. 1991.)

Frances Stevenson Wein, Editor, *National Portrait Gallery, Smithsonian Institution, Permanent Collection Illustrated Checklist*, Published for the National Portrait Gallery by the Smithsonian Institution Press, City of Washington, 1982.

Frank F. White, Jr., *The Governors of Maryland: 1771-1970*, Publication No. 15, The Hall of Records Commission, State of Maryland, Annapolis, 1970, Twentieth Century Printing Co., Inc., 406 West Redwood Street, Baltimore, Maryland 21201.

The World Book Encyclopedia, (Chicago-London-Rome-Sydney-Toronto: Field Enterprises Educational Corporation, 1968), Volume 20.

Addendum C
University and Library
Special Collections Examined

American Antiquarian Society, Worcester, Massachusetts.

Thomas Balch Library, 208 W. Market Street, Leesburg, Virginia.

Central Rappahannock Regional Library, The Wallace Library, 1201 Caroline Street, Fredericksburg, Virginia.

Charles County, Maryland, Clerk of the Court and Register of Wills Offices, Charles County Courthouse, La Plata, Maryland.

The College of William and Mary, Earl Gregg Swem Library, Williamsburg, Virginia.

Department of the Interior, National Park Service, Edwin Bearrs, Chief Historian, Washington, D. C.

Descendants of the Signers of the Declaration of Independence, Ridley Park, Pennsylvania.

Dickinson College Library, Carlisle, Pennsylvania.

Easton Public Library, History Room, 2245 Fairview Ave., Easton, Pennsylvania.

East Texas State University, Commerce, Texas.

The Historical Society of Delaware, 505 Market Street Mall, Wilmington, Delaware.

Johns Hopkins University, The Milton S. Eisenhower Library, 3400 N. Charles Street, Baltimore, Maryland.

Independence Hall Museum, Philadelphia, Pennsylvania.

Kenyon College, Department of Anthropology and Sociology, Bailey House (Howard L. Sacks), Gambier, Ohio.

Lafayette College, David Bishop Skillman Library, Easton, Pennsylvania.

Latter Day Saints Family Genealogy Center, 35 N. West Temple Street, Temple Square, Salt Lake City, Utah.

Lauinger Library, Georgetown University Special Collections, Washington, DC

Maryland Courts of Appeal, Law Library, Rowe Blvd., Annapolis, Maryland.

Massachusetts Historical Society, 1154 Boylston Street, Boston, Massachusetts.

James Monroe Museum, Charles Street, Fredericksburg, Virginia.

National Geographic Society, 17th Street, N. W., Room 816, Washington, D. C.

National Park Service, Independence National Historical Park, Philadelphia, Pennsylvania.

The New Jersey Historical Society, 230 Broadway, Newark, New Jersey.

Northampton County Historical Society, Easton, Pennsylvania.

Paris Junior College, 2400 Clarksville St., Paris, Texas.

Porter Historical Society, Youngstown, New York.

Princeton Monthly Meeting (Quaker) at Stony Brook, Rivendell, 599 Pretty Brook Road, Princeton, New Jersey.

Princeton University History Project, Institute for Historic Research, 221 Nassau, Princeton, New Jersey.

Randolph-Macon Women's College, Lynchburg, Virginia.
St. Johns College Library, Annapolis, Maryland.
Salisbury State University, Edward H. Nabb Research Center for Delmarva
        History, Salisbury, Maryland.
San Diego County (California) Clerk of the Court, Office of Wills, San Diego,
        California.
San Diego Museum of Art, Balboa Park, San Diego, California.
San Francisco State University, Sutro Genealogy Library, San Francisco,
        California.
Seattle Main Library, Special Collections, Seattle, Washington.
Sons of the American Revolution, 1000 S. 4th Street, Louisville, Kentucky.
Southern Illinois University, Morris Library, Special Collections, Carbondale,
        Illinois.
State of Arizona, Department of Library, Archives and Public Records, 1700
        W. Washington, Phoenix, Arizona.
University of North Carolina, Library, Special Collections, Chapel Hill, North
        Carolina.
University of Virginia Library, Charlottesville, Virginia.
The Virginia Historical Society, Battle Abbey, Richmond, Virginia.
Virginia State Library, Eleventh Street and Capital Square, Richmond,
        Virginia.
Washington University Libraries, Olin Library System, Campus Box 1061,
        St. Louis, Missouri.

Addendum D
Paper and People Trails

Often in works of history the tales of how writers seek credible sources of information constitute an important part of the product itself. We began our work about two centuries after the death of Thomas Stone. Historiographical research paths grow quite cold during two hundred years. Pertinent factors bearing on Stone research follow –

- Size of the broad Stone family community in the colonies – different branches in different sections not necessarily related.
- Failure of Stone's family to gather and preserve his personal papers after his death. Even well into the 20th Century Stone family papers were entering special collections in library systems of several United States' institutions of academia.
- Stone research even extended to locating possible letters of pertinent materials offered by major New York auction galleries. In 1967 Parke-Bernet Galleries, Inc. announced for sale a "distinguished private collection" of letters and documents attributed to Signers of the Declaration of Independence. Of special interest to us was a Thomas Stone letter of April 13, 1783 to his brother, Walter. In referring to the Declaration of Independence Stone commented:

   . . . We have received the long wished official information [Treaty of Paris] *of a general peace being concluded at which we all most heartily rejoice. We must now set earnestly about paying our public debt . . . and lay the foundation of happiness and liberty to posterity .* . . [167]

   This letter marks Stone as a very happy man to be a citizen of the new nation he helped create against incredible odds.
- Fortunately some passionate 19th Century autograph collectors, recognizing as early as the 1830's the rarity of the Thomas Stone signature, acquired several important letters and commercial papers signed by Stone. These were located in repositories coast to coast.
- Stone family document (primary sources) collections of any significant size were at Duke University, Library of Congress, Maryland Historical Society and Maryland's Hall of Records.
- A search for the Robert Edge Pine 1785 oil portraits of Margaret and Thomas Stone began in Easton, Pennsylvania about 1985. We discovered that the paintings had left Fredericksburg, Virginia about 1860 when philologist Professor Francis Andrew March traveled north

---

167 Parke-Bernet Galleries, Inc., 980 Madison Ave., New York, New York. Sale Nr. 2569, May 16, 1967

to assume a very prestigious staff position at Lafayette College. His wife, Margaret Mildred Conway, granddaughter of Margaret Stone Daniel, had brought the paintings to Easton. With her only brother deceased and being the older of the two Stone girls Margaret had logically inherited these priceless works. A descendant of Margaret Mildred Conway March inherited these paintings and, while living in Youngstown, New York, about 1950, donated them to the National Portrait Gallery. We had traced them to her western New York home at the time that she and the Gallery were negotiating the transfer of the Pine portraits to a proper, secure home in perpetuity. [168] Thomas Stone portrait was a **copy** (likely done by a Pine family member just before 1800). The Signer's wife's Pine portrait was a 1785 original. They are now possessed by the National Portrait Gallery in Washington, D. C. [169] The Thomas 1785 original hung in the

---

168   Robert G. Stewart, *Robert Edge Pine, A British Portrait Painter in America,* (Washington, D.C.: National Portrait Gallery, Smithsonian Institution Press, 1979). Pine was a somewhat tragic figure. He left his native England late in 1784 because of his unhappy lot in the British art community, a result of politics and prejudice of some of England's most distinguished painters, including Sir Joshua Reynolds – known as "Painter to the King." Pine on the other hand had spoken many times in sympathy with the cause of America's revolution against the Crown. In fact, Pine desired to come to America to do portraits of all the patriot leaders of this war. Such men and such feelings were not welcome at Court. After Pine and family settled in Philadelphia late in 1784 he planned a trip to Mount Vernon early the next year to begin his ambitious work by having George Washington sit for him. The General already had received laudatory letters of introduction from mutual friends in England.

After a successful experience at Mount Vernon Pine traveled to Annapolis in a coach furnished by an impressed Washington. Most likely the Stone sittings took place about mid-1785 at their Peggy Stewart house on Hanover Street. The Stones, both still youthful, had only two years more to live.

With respect to any conjectural appraisal of the quality and accuracy of Pine's Stone portraits, an old friend of Washington commented that the artist's portrait of the General " . . . bore the strongest resemblance to the original [real life Washington] of any I had seen." These were the words of Catherine MacCauley Graham.

169   Frances Stevenson Wine, ed., *National Portrait Gallery, Permanent Collection Illustrated Checklist,* 1982 Edition. Acquisitions through September 30, 1981 (Washington, D.C.: Smithsonian Institution Press, 1982), page 218.

Thomas Stone the Signer. Copy of Robert Edge Pine's portrait painted in mid-1785. Only about this much of the painting was done at Annapolis and carried by Pine to his Philadelphia studio where the rest of the portrait was added. Restored by the National Portrait Gallery after its acquisition. This is an extremely faithful copy of that portrait. Art historians feel it was done before 1800 in Philadelphia after Pine's death by an obviously very accomplished painter in Pine's family — possibly a daughter. Margaret Stone's original was acquired and restored at the same time. No copy of Margaret's portrait is known to exist.

National Portrait Gallery, Smithsonian Institution. Gift of Mrs. Frank J. Clement
(nee March), a fifth generation descendant of Thomas and Margaret Stone.

magnificently paneled parlor of Habre de Venture under the care of four generations of the Stone family occupants. This Pine portrait was sold to the Baltimore Museum of Art in 1927 with the paneling from the parlor.

- Another research adventure issued from a 1986 taped interview with the late Colonel Frederick Stone Matthews, U.S.A., then living in Baltimore. After receiving a Reserve Officer Training Corps commission at St. John's College in Annapolis about 1912 Colonel Matthews joined the United States Army and saw active duty in General John Pershing's 1915-17 border crusade against the shifty, shadowy Pancho Villa along both sides of the Rio Grande River. During World War I he commanded Maryland militia on railroad security missions. Then, many years later, Colonel Matthews saw much active duty in World War II in France as head of G-1 (Personnel) on the staff of General George Patton.

Colonel Matthews was born near Port Tobacco, Maryland on October 10, 1892. He died in Baltimore on May 28, 1998 – five months before his 106th birthday. He is notable in our story because he possessed the original Thomas Stone gold signet ring, a Stone artifact easily attributed to the Signer. Before the Colonel and his two daughters donated this ring to the Maryland Historical Society we were allowed to see it and make wax impressions from it. Had the Signer's son Frederick survived the 1793 yellow fever horror he doubtless would have received the ring.

Our calculated generational descent of this ring:
Judge-Congressman Michael Jenifer Stone; his son
Frederick Daniel Stone; his son
Judge Frederick Stone (1820-1899), also a Congressman and member of the State Court of Appeals; (this Frederick had no male issue); his oldest daughter, Jennie, married
John Matthews about 1890; their first born child was Frederick Stone Matthews. And he inherited the truly magnificent, tastefully executed gold signet ring of the Signer.

- Because of leads at Richmond's Battle Abbey about 1987 we did some work in 1991 in San Diego and studied the will of Miss Mary Vivian Conway a great-great granddaughter of Thomas and Margaret, and something of a family historian. She based her claim for membership in the Descendants of Signers of the Declaration of Independence partly on her ascendency from the Stones of Habre de Venture. Mary Vivian, who never married, died in 1953 in possession of several Stone family artifacts that she claimed had been in Habre de Venture, including a silver candelabra.

- We found that at least a half dozen Stone-Daniel descendants fought for the Confederacy. One of these, a grandson of Margaret Stone Daniel (Mrs. John Moncure Daniel, doctor), was James Mitchell

Daniel who helped found Paris, Texas about 1855 and then served the Confederacy as a Captain of artillery. His daughter, Mary Vivian Daniel, another Stone family historian who upon her death left a rich trove of family history notes and photos. In this mass of research findings was one of the finest collections of Stone-Daniel family photos ever seen. The most impressive is a ferrotype copy of an excellent painting c.1790 of Dr. John Moncure Daniel, son-in-law of Margaret and Thomas Stone. The whereabouts of this painting is a mystery.

- An odd and interesting sidelight of our 1991 visit to the San Diego Museum of Art was the discovery of a superlative oil portrait of a granddaughter of Port Tobacco's Habre de Venture Stones on display in the Fine Arts Collection. The vivid color in this large canvas is an eye opener. The painting was executed by Maryland's foremost 19th Century woman painter, Sarah Miriam Peale (1800-1885). Probably it was done during her Baltimore years (1823-47). The subject was Mrs. William Crane (Jean Niven Daniel, who became the wife about 1825 of Baltimore merchant, William Crane) who lived here at this time. Mrs. Crane was a daughter of the Stone's older daughter, Margaret. Throughout her life she remained intensely proud of her descent from the youngest Maryland Signer. She and her children were the only descendants of Thomas Stone living in Maryland in the 19th Century. The museum's attribution for this work was totally inadequate – even erroneous in some ways. They knew that it was a work of Sarah Miriam Peale and that the subject was Mrs. William Crane of Baltimore. They did not know that Mrs. Crane was a granddaughter of Signer Thomas and Margaret Stone. The painting had been donated to the museum about 1950 by Mary Vivian Conway of San Diego who was a great-great granddaughter of the Stones.

Painting of Jean Niven Daniel Crane by Sarah Miriam Peale. Painting hangs in San Diego Museum of Art in Balboa Park. Given to museum by Mary Vivian Conway about 1952. Miss Conway was a great grand daughter of Margaret and Thomas Stone of Habre de Venture. Mrs. Crane was a grand daughter of Margaret and Thomas Stone.

- We knew early in our search that the two Stone girls left Maryland forever when they married brothers in Stafford County's (Virginia) Daniel family. Several direct descendants of the two Stone-Daniel unions have been traced by us. An amazingly sophisticated and creative group of them had distinguished careers up through the early years of this century, especially the children of Professor and Mrs. Francis Andrew March of Easton, Pennsylvania – an Army General, one college professor, a journalist, a lawyer and a public school superintendent.

Perhaps one of the most distinguished fourth generation achievers was General Peyton Conway March, who was General Pershing's commander during World War I. He had command responsibility for all U. S. troops in France. March may be described as the General George Marshall of World War I. United States Air Force's March Field in California was named after this descendant.

The Mildred Stone Conway and Francis Andrew March, Sr. family of Easton, PA. Standing, left to right — John Lewis born 1873, Alden born 1869, Peyton Conway born 1864, Thomas Stone born 1868, Moncure born 1868. Seated left to right — Mildred Margaret born 1875, Francis Andrew, Jr. born 1863, Francis Andrew, Sr. born 1825, died 1911, Margaret Mildred Stone Conway born 1837, died 1911, Margaret Daniel born 1877. Note the remarkable resemblance between Thomas Stone and five members in this C 1900 photo of the March family.

Habre de Venture is on Rose Hill Road between MD Routes 6 and 225 near Port Tobacco. The site is open from 9 a.m. - 5 p.m., Wed. - Sun., September through May. It is open daily during June, July and August. Exhibits, tours and a video presentation are available. The Thomas Stone National Historic Site is located thirty miles south of Washington, DC.

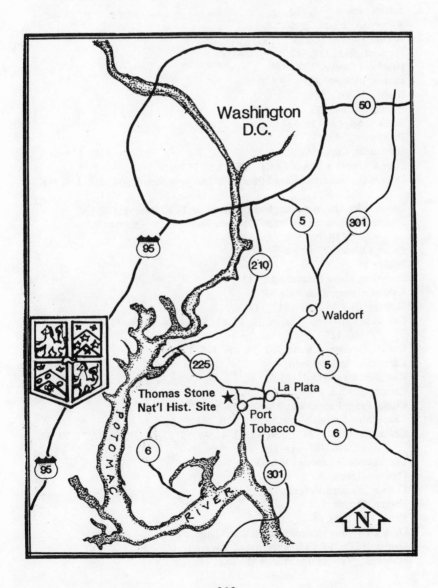

Index

215